LESLIE BECK™

Best *of the* Best
Quilts

Landauer Books

Leslie Beck's
Best of the Best Quilts

Copyright© 2002 by Landauer Corporation
Projects Copyright© 2002 by Fiber Mosaics

This book was designed, produced, and published by Landauer Books
A division of Landauer Corporation
12251 Maffitt Road, Cumming, Iowa 50061

President/Publisher: Jeramy Lanigan Landauer
Executive Vice President Sales & Marketing: James L. Knapp
Executive Vice President Editorial: Becky Johnston
Creative Director: Laurel Albright
Project Editor: M. Peg Smith
Editorial Coordinator: Kimberly O'Brien
Production Manager: Linda Bender
Technical Illustrators: Sarah Bendy, Marcia Cameron, Barb Gordon
Production Artist: Pat Seifert
Photographer: Craig Anderson Photography

ISBN: 1-890621-41-2
This book printed on acid-free paper.
Printed in China.

10-9-8-7-6-5-4-3-2-1

Introduction

Leslie Beck and her creative staff draw inspiration for casual living from the fibers of life and textures of nature. With evergrowing recognizable designs in fabrics, quilts, and home decor, Leslie and her innovative team received a Tommy Award in 1996—an industry mark of excellence.

The 36 quilts in this collection—folk art with a contemporary twist to sophisticated country—emphasize color, shape, and texture for versatile and timeless appeal.

Quilts

A Brief Review of Quilt Blocks in America

Although quilting in one form or another had been practiced for centuries throughout Europe and Asia, American quilters developed a unique style that reflected the culture and spirit of the country. Earliest quilts were an interpretation of needlework traditions that women brought with them, typically whole cloth quilts. Soon after, quilts were made from blocks that were pieced using one, two, or several fabrics. Blocks became a truly American style, often created through necessity and inspired by nature. Blocks, sewn together in myriad settings, then layered with backing and filling, provided warmth, an artistic outlet, and, importantly, a record of the American Heritage.

In the spirit of "Use it up, wear it out, make it do, or do without," American quilters to the new frontier combined fabrics with sentiment and function. The pieced designs that grew from this diverse group of people who settled in and traversed the country provide a history of travels, hardship, celebration, and patriotism.

Some of the projects in this book are the result of inspiration from quilters years ago. By incorporating historical designs, the tradition of piecing and quilting is passed along to new generations. A bit of history is recorded through each new quilt that is made and shared. Future generations will determine which colors, patterns, and styles were integral to the time period and which events influenced the lives of the quilters.

Some prevalent block designs provide a basis for beginners, novices, and avid quilters alike to experiment with color and design. We are forever grateful to our foremothers for creating and passing along these, as well as other, well-known designs that quilters will continue to cherish.

Log Cabin—

An all-time favorite since the mid-1800s, this humble block is associated with Abraham Lincoln's presidential campaign. Symbolic of the American frontier, the blocks are assembled in a multitude of arrangements—such as Barn Raising, Straight Furrows, Streak of Lightning, Medallion, and Sunshine and Shadow, as well as many other designs. Successively longer strips of fabric are sewn clockwise around a center square as if building a cabin of logs.

Often center squares are a single, unifying color, with yellow representing a welcoming glow from windows and red the hearth of the home. During the Civil War, Log Cabin quilts with black center squares were hung on clotheslines to indicate that they were Underground Railroad stations and whether it was safe to enter (there is also a quilt pattern called Underground Railroad).

Log Cabin block designs have thrived through times of fabric scarcity and abundance. When fabric was scarce, quilters salvaged worn clothing to cut and store strips. The versatility of the strips made this an economical method; strips were sewn to a center block, trimmed to size, and the remaining strip could be used elsewhere. Utilitarian quilts made from these blocks were used daily by family members. As the quilts became worn, they often were enclosed in newer utilitarian quilts as added warmth.

Log Cabin Variation

Four-Patch and Nine-Patch—

These blocks also were the result of the frugal use of fabrics when fabric was scarce or to meet the necessity of utilitarian quilts. Patch blocks were often taught to young girls as they pieced their first quilts, often at the ages of 10 or 11. During plentiful times, fabrics were combined to make color variations of Four-Patch and Nine-Patch. These blocks are the foundation for such block designs as Irish Chain and Burgoyne Surrounded, both of which reflect significant cultural events of the United States.

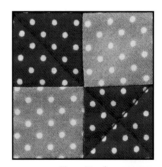

Four-Patch

Nine-Patch

7

Bear's Paw—

As the name indicates, this block depicts the fascination with the New Frontier and was a way for pioneer women to connect the adventure of the time with the warmth of the home. The blocks are made with squares and half-square triangles and can be set in a variety of pleasing arrangements or included in sampler quilts.

Bear Paw

Courthouse Steps—

A version of the Log Cabin block, this block differs in that successively longer strips are sewn to opposite sides of the center square. One theory for the design suggests a balance of just laws, weighing the evidence before making a fair decision. Similar to the Log Cabin, Courthouse Steps can be arranged in delightfully colorful settings that create movement in a quilt.

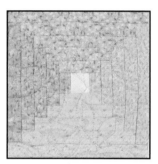

Courthouse Steps

Sawtooth Star—

Fascination with the skies and travel through the wilderness may be the inspiration for blocks that resemble stars, which are made in miniature or as large center blocks. The pattern is frequently used in sampler quilts and is charming in color combinations from bright to homespun plaid.

Sawtooth or Ohio Star

Flying Geese—

Used in bold borders, repeated in quilt top rows, or as points for Star blocks, Flying Geese is as popular today as it was to quilters who witnessed large honking geese flying overhead. Nature inspired, and sometimes frustrated, the women of the frontier and early settlements, who incorporated what they saw in their daily lives into useful objects.

Flying Geese Border

FABRIC

Choose light- to medium-weight 100-percent-cotton fabrics. Use fabrics with a tight weave to prevent distortion while cutting and sewing and for a smooth, professional-looking finish. Avoid fabrics that are loosely woven or appear overly stiff. As a guide, within a quilt project, select compatible fabric textures.

Washing fabrics before cutting them is purely an individual choice; however, it is strongly recommended that all fabrics for quilting be preshrunk. Some quilters prefer to wash fabrics for softness and to remove excess dye and sizing. Before washing in the washing machine, cut raw edges with a pinking shears or wavy rotary blade to prevent loose threads from tangling, or sew a basting stitch along long raw edges. Enclose small fabric pieces in a mesh bag to prevent tangling and twisting in the washer. Wash similar colors together in cool or warm water to prevent dyes bleeding from one fabric to another, use a mild detergent (or quilter's soap) and delicate or normal wash cycle. Fabric also may be washed by hand in a sink or tub, which allows you to see how much dye bleeds from the fabric so that several rinses can be repeated (if fabric continues to bleed after numerous rinsing, do not use it in a quilt). Either hang the wet fabrics to damp dry over plastic hangers and press them dry with a steam iron, or tumble them lightly before pressing. If you prefer a finish with body for cutting and piecing, spray the fabric with sizing as you press. Fold the fabric pieces over hangers to keep them crisp and fresh until ready to cut.

If you prefer not to prewash fabrics, you must be aware that some shrinkage will occur and some bleeding of dyes may occur when the quilt is washed. Some quilters prefer the soft look of the gentle puckers between blocks as fabrics shrink slightly in the stitched quilt. Quilted wall hangings, which may only require light vacuuming or shaking, are projects that do not necessitate prewashed fabrics. The preference is yours to make for each project.

CUTTING TOOLS

Store tools at or near your sewing machine in a well-organized box or kit. Finding the right tool at the right time saves time and frustration as you work on projects.

- Rotary cutter—Use a size and design that fits your hand and that has a lock to cover the blade when it is not in use. Keep an extra blade on hand to change during projects to avoid cutting fabrics with a dull blade.

- Acrylic ruler—Use a ruler that has 1/4" and 1/8" marks, and diagonal (30°, 45°, and 60°) as well as horizontal and vertical rules. Available in several dimensions and designs, a standard 6×24" ruler will work well for most projects. Square rulers are handy for squaring blocks and other uses.

- Self-healing cutting mat—An 18×24" mat, with 1" gridded squares, is standard and will accommodate cutting a large piece of fabric while fitting on most flat, stable surfaces. Place the mat at a comfortable height for cutting, reaching, and folding fabric.

- Scissors:

  Fabric-cutting—Reserve one pair of scissors for cutting fabric *only*.

  Utilitarian—Use a second pair or scissors to cut paper patterns and template plastic.

  Optional—Small scissors with sharp points, thread nippers, embroidery scissors, or a seam ripper are beneficial for cutting notches, getting into tight spots, and removing threads.

MARKING TOOLS

Test marking tools on scrap fabric to determine whether they are safe to use on fabric in your projects. Store a variety of these tools close to the machine for frequent use.

- Chalk, washable graphite, silver, or white pencil—to show on dark fabrics but that will not leave a permanent mark.

- Erasers—To erase on paper and fabrics; use large, soft erasers.

- Fine-grit sandpaper—One sheet of fine-grit sandpaper holds fabric pieces in place for marking and prevents the distortion that might occur when pulling a pencil lead across a smooth surface.

- Pencils—use sharp, hard-lead pencils to mark fabric patterns and quilting designs; use sharp No. 2 pencils to trace around patterns onto paper or webbing.

- Permanent marking tools that do not bleed—to make labels to sew to the back of quilts.

- Quilter's mechanical pencil with either medium or medium hard (0.5) lead refills—to mark fabrics and draw on paper.

SEWING TOOLS

- Sewing machine and accessories—Straight-stitch sewing machines are sufficient for most quilting projects; however, for machine appliqué, a tight zigzag stitch is required.

  1/4" foot—although not necessary, a specially designed 1/4" sewing machine foot is helpful for making accurate seams. If your machine does not have one, generic brands are available that may fit, or you can make a guide to use with your machine. Measure 1/4" from the needle and place a tape marker at the point. Stitch a seam, with the raw edge of the seam along the mark, and measure it for accuracy. Adjust the mark as necessary to get an accurate 1/4" seam allowance. It is critical to sew accurate seams when piecing.

  Walking foot or even-feed foot—For machine quilting without puckers on the backside of the quilt and to sew on binding, these feet are useful accessories. Check available accessories for your machine to determine whether this is an option.

- Pins and pincushion or pinholder—Use good quality, rustproof, long quilter's pins for piecing and appliqué. Colorful round or glass heads are easy to see and grasp. Use long pins to guide fabric under the needle when sewing small pieces. Stuffed or magnetic pincushions make it easy to keep track of pins and prevent spilling.

- Safety pins—Use brass or nickel-coated safety pins (size 1 is recommended) to hold quilt layers together for machine quilting. Approximately 350 to 500 1"-long safety pins, spaced approximately 6" apart, would be required to baste a large quilt for machine quilting.

- Needles:

  Sewing machine—Size 80 is recommended for most cotton fabrics. Use high-quality sewing machine needles that fit the machine, thread, and fabrics. Change needles with each project to avoid them breaking and/or pulling and distorting the fabric. A new needle often solves a variety of stitching problems. Don't compromise quality for price on needles.

  Hand-stitching—

  Betweens—The smaller the number the larger the needle. Quilters develop a preference for sizes for specific projects, although the following is a guide: Nos. 7 to 9 for basting, Nos. 10 to 12 for hand-quilting, and Nos. 11 or 12 for handsewing and appliqué.

  Sharps—Use these all-purpose sewing needles for appliqué or patchwork.

- Thread—Use cotton or cotton-covered polyester sewing thread; polyester threads can cut into cotton fibers. Basic threads for quilting include neutrals, such as white, tan, or medium gray to blend with a variety of fabrics. When sewing on a two-color quilt project, you may wish to choose a thread that blends with one or both colors; otherwise, using a neutral that blends with most colors saves time from changing threads.

- Thimble—Such a wide variety of styles and materials are used for thimbles that it is a matter of personal preference. Select from metal, plastic, or leather for a snug-fitting, but not tight, thimble that fits your middle finger. Use a thimble not only to protect your fingers from needle pokes but also to protect the project from blood spots.

- Quilting hoop—14–18" circular hand-held or tabletop wooden hoops are portable, easy to use, and take little storage space. The size is adequate for quilting even a large quilt top. Hoops made of wood, metal, and plastic are available in round, oval, and half rounds in larger and smaller sizes.

PRESSING TOOLS

- Iron, ironing board, and press cloth—Pressing after each sewing step is critical to the finished project. Press fabric by holding a steam or dry iron over the fabric without sliding. Sliding an iron over fabric, especially diagonal or bias seams, distorts them. Even though a slight difference in one piece may seem negligible, when the pieces are joined to make a quilt top, the problem may be compounded. Take care in pressing seams with steam if you have not preshrunk the fabric.

  Press the seam flat to set the stitches. Then press the seam in the direction of the darker fabric or in the direction of least resistance. When pressing small or delicate pieces, use a press cloth.

MISCELLANEOUS TOOLS

- Template plastic—Trace patterns to template plastic and cut with utilitarian scissors to use for cutting multiples of the same shape. Using plastic or vinyl rather than paper maintains a clean and uniform edge to the pattern pieces.

- Tracing paper—Keep a pad of tracing paper with your sewing supplies to use to trace patterns and make templates.

Appliqué—visible or invisible stitching that secures a piece of fabric to a background. Appliqué is done by hand or machine with contrasting or coordinating thread, with fabric edges turned under or flat, depending on the finished design. Fusible webbing is often used to secure fabric layers together.

Backing—The backside of the quilt. Choose backing fabric compatible with the quilt top. For example, all-cotton backings are appropriate for all-cotton quilt tops. Prewash the backing if the fabric for quilt top is prewashed to prevent excessive puckering when the quilt is laundered. Backing fabric is usually pieced for large quilts, using all one fabric or an assortment of pieced fabrics for an interesting or artistic look. The backing fabric, pieced or whole, should extend approximately 5 inches in each direction beyond the quilt top. The backing is laid wrong side up on a smooth, flat surface, the batting is laid over the backing, and the quilt top is laid face up over the two layers. The layers are smoothed and pinned and/or basted to hold them together for quilting or tying. After the quilting is complete, the backing is trimmed even with the quilt top. Binding is sewn through all layers and turned to the backside and stitched in place.

Batting—The layer between the quilt top and backing that provides warmth and dimension. Choose from polyester, cotton, wool, and fusible batting appropriate for the project. Polyester batts are lightweight and have loft for fullness; some types may "beard," which means that fibers are brought to the quilt surface while quilting. Cotton batts adhere well to cotton fabrics, require more rows of stitching than polyester to prevent bunching when they are washed, have less loft than polyester, and provide a natural look. Wool batts are more expensive than polyester and cotton; they absorb moisture, have some loft, and are warm. They can be washed on gentle cycle and air-dried to prevent shrinkage. Fusible batting is low-loft polyester used for wall hangings, home décor projects, and some quilts to eliminate pinning or basting. Fusing washes out when laundered (refer to manufacturer instructions for fiber content and appropriate use).

To layer batting, allow approximately 5 inches extension on all sides of large quilts and 2 inches on small quilts to compensate for stitching. After quilting, trim batting even with the quilt top and bind.

Bias—The diagonal of woven fabric. Bias is more flexible than straight or crosswise grain. Fabric is cut on the bias to ease around corners and form free-form designs, such as in binding and appliquéd vines.

Binding—The finished edge of the quilt that encloses the layers. Fabric strips are cut, joined in a continuous length, pressed, folded in half lengthwise, wrong sides together, and pressed. The raw edge of the binding is placed against the raw edge of the quilt top and sewn on with a 1/4" seam allowance. Where the binding rounds a corner, the binding is mitered for a clean finish on the front and back. The long edges of the binding are either overlapped to enclose raw edges or joined in a seam for a continuous binding finish. After the binding is sewn all around the quilt top, it is folded to the backside of the quilt and handsewn in place with a blind- or hemstitch.

Chain-piecing—Streamlined sewing by continuously feeding small pieces under the presser foot to join several units before lifting the presser foot and cutting the thread. Use this method, for example, when sewing Log Cabin strips around a center block, sewing all the same-size strips to the same side of each block. If necessary, use a long straight pin to help feed fabric, such as triangle corners and small pieces, under the presser foot. After the pieces are joined, lift the presser foot and cut the thread nearest the needle. Remove the chained units, clip the threads between each unit, press, and open the fabric pieces.

Fusible webbing—Double-sided light-, medium-, or heavy-weight adhesive for fusing fabrics together, or strengthening and stabilizing fabrics for appliqué. The fusing adhesive is activated by applying a hot, dry iron. Paper covering on one side of the fusing material allows for tracing and cutting designs to apply to the wrong side of fabric. Choose the appropriate weight of fusing material for the fabrics and follow manufacturer's directions for tracing, cutting, and fusing the adhesive to fabric.

Grain—Lengthwise and crosswise woven fabric threads. Look at the weave of the fabric. Lengthwise threads run parallel to the selvage and crosswise threads run from selvage to selvage. Grain is more obvious, for example, in homespun or open weaves than in polished cotton or tight weaves.

Press—Use an iron set on cotton and either dry or steam. Press with the iron for a few seconds and lift without sliding. (If fabric is not preshrunk, use care with steam.) Avoid sliding the iron across fabric and seams, which pulls or distorts fabric, especially bias seams and bias-cut pieces. Pressing after each piecing stage to keep units and blocks uniform for a neat finished project. Press seams flat to set them before pressing in one direction. Use a press cloth to anchor pieces when pressing small units or several bias seams. Project directions usually indicate which direction to press the seam. When several seams cross, press in the direction of least resistance or toward the darkest fabric. For flat finishes, press seams that will abut with an adjacent seam (as in block rows), in opposite directions. When rows are joined, align stitching lines and allow the seam allowances to fall in opposite directions.

Selvage—The manufactured edges of the fabric, often with printing that indicates the manufacturer and colors. Remove selvage edges from the fabric before making final cuts; do not include them in sewing projects as they may pucker or weaken the finished project.

Strip—Refers to cutting across the fabric from selvage to selvage (42" long) for the project width. Strips are then cut to size or sewn together.

Template-free angle piecing—Use this method to join right-angle units with a diagonal seam (such as Flying Geese units) to eliminate difficult to sew angles and for a neat finish. Usually a small square is sewn to a larger piece and the seam of the smaller piece *only* is trimmed before pressing the unit.

BACKING, BATTING, BASTING, QUILTING, AND BINDING

After the quilt top has been pieced and pressed, mark a quilting design using quilter's pencils or chalk, if desired; then put the layers together. If quilting in the ditch or along straight lines, use narrow masking tape or guide the stitches by sight after the quilt top, batting, and backing are layered.

1. Piece the backing fabric (if necessary) using a 1/2" seam allowance, using the same fabric or combining fabrics for a designed back. Backing pieces should be from 5" to 10" larger all around than the quilt top to allow for stitching and complete coverage. Press the seams in one direction.

2. Lay the backing fabric on a smooth, flat surface with the right side of the fabric facing the surface. Use masking tape or weights to secure the fabric and hold it smooth.

3. Unwrap the batting and allow it to loft for several hours or squirt with water and place in a dryer for 5 minutes. If necessary trim the batting to approximately the same size as the backing, at least 5" to 10" larger all around than the quilt top. Layer the batting on the backing fabric.

4. If the quilt top has bias edges, stay-stitch close to the edge (1/8") to prevent stretching. Center the quilt top face up on the batting, and smooth it evenly.

5. Use rustproof safety pins to secure the quilt top to the layers beneath. Either pin closely throughout the quilt top, or use the pins to secure the layers while basting the layers together.

6. To baste the layers, use a long needle and lengths of thread to baste from the center to each corner and each edge of the quilt top, using long (1/2" to 2") stitches, depending on the quilt size and batting loft. The larger the quilt top, the more radiating basting stitches to use. For successive lines of stitching from the center to the edges, baste directly from center for the first lines and stitch farther from center for successive lines.

7. As the quilt top is hand- or machine-quilted, remove the basting pins or basting threads. Long basting threads can be removed after the quilting is complete unless they hinder the quilting.

8. After quilting, lay the quilt top flat and trim the backing and batting even with the quilt top.

9. Prepare the binding. Sew lengths together with bias seams for a continuous binding length to fit the circumference of the quilt top plus approximately 12" extension. (Cutting instructions for binding width and length are included with each project.) Fold the continuous binding strip in half lengthwise, wrong sides together, matching long raw edges. Press the strip.

10. Beginning approximately one-fourth of the way from a side or bottom corner of the quilt top, place the raw edge of the binding against the raw edge of the quilt top, allowing approximately 6" of binding to be free. Leaving the free end of binding, pin and stitch the binding to the quilt top. Stitch 1/4" seam, stitching in a straight line toward the first corner.

11. Stop stitching 1/4" from the corner, backstitch, slide the quilt top away from the feed dogs, and clip the thread. Fold the binding back on itself to create a 90 degree angle, hold the binding

against the previous edge sewn, and fold it forward, matching raw edges along the adjacent quilt top edge, and creating a tuck in the binding at the corner of the quilt top. Place the fabric under the foot, put the needle down along the top raw edge and folded binding, and stitch to within 1/4" of the next corner. Sew the binding to the quilt top until approximately 10" from the beginning stitching.

12. Remove the quilt top from the machine. Adjust the free binding edges to the remaining length of the quilt top. Sew the binding edges together and trim the excess seam allowance. Match and sew the binding to the quilt top edge.

13. Fold the binding to the backside of the quilt and hand-stitch it in place along the fold of the binding, using matching thread and nearly invisible stitches.

14. Sew a label to the back of the quilt with your name and date as well as other pertinent information if it is a gift.

15. If the quilt is a gift, include a care card. Indicate how to fold for storage (refolding every few weeks to prevent permanent creases), launder with quilt soap and cool water, and to dry on delicate cycle to fluff and to finish by air drying.

EMBROIDERY STITCHES

Back Stitch

French Knot

Satin Stitch

Buttonhole Stitch

Machine Satin Stitching

Cross Stitch

Running Stitch

Stem Stitch

Dedication

To my husband, Byron Sr., and my children,
Byron Jr., Christine, and Kate, who have always
believed in me, supported me, and urged me forward.
With their love and patience, I have been able
to pursue my design career.

This book also is dedicated to quilters everywhere.
I sincerely hope that you will be inspired by
our *Best of the Best* and will create
treasured memories to use and share.

Acknowledgments

The *Best of the Best* is a compilation of refined techniques, trend-setting styles,
and traditional quilts. Acknowledgment and thanks to my team of dedicated artists and editors:

Retta Warehime, quilt designer and author. She has led the team
through many hours of cutting, measuring, sewing, writing, and editing.

Debbie Baalman and Shirley Christensen, excellent piecers and quilters.

Special recognition to Patty Wagner, Byron Beck,
and Earlene Sullivan for the computer graphics and text.

Pam Clarke and Debbie Cole, whose quilting designs add an
extraordinary enhancement to the designs, creating truly distinctive quilts.

I am ever grateful for the guidance and encouragement from Becky Johnston.
With her vision, along with the Landauer team, the *Best of the Best* became reality.

Cape Cod

Like sails scurrying across the water, these crisp plaid triangles recall summer days spent at a cool, breezy lake.

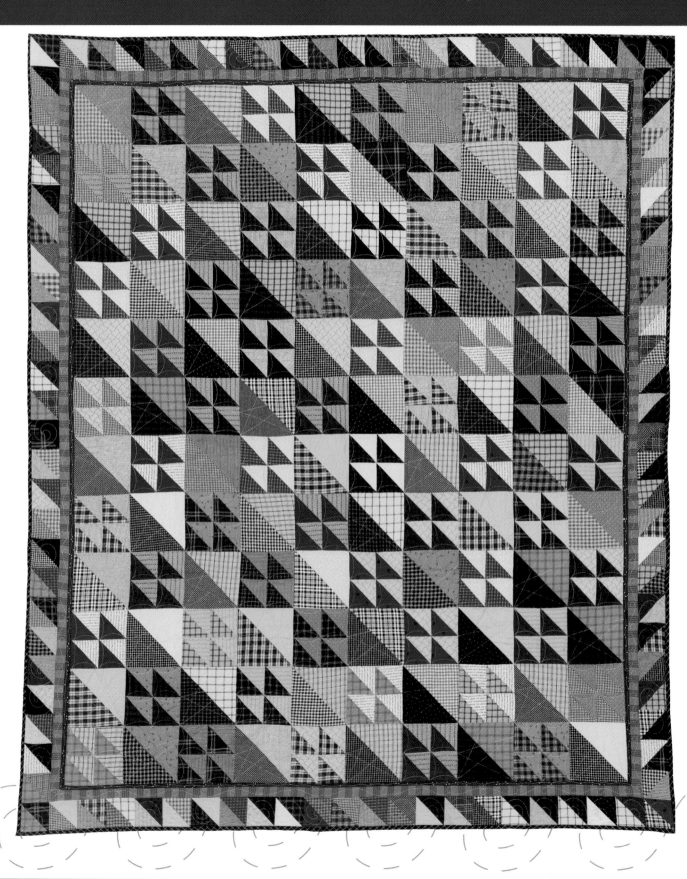

Finished size 69×81"
Finished blocks 6" square

Select the fabric

*1/3 yard each of 20 assorted fabrics
for small triangle squares*

*1/3 yard each of 16 assorted fabrics
for large triangle squares*

1/3 yard for red accent border

1/2 yard for gold accent border

2/3 yard for binding

4-1/4 yards for backing

Cut the fabric

1. From each fabric for small half-square triangles, cut
   1—9" strip; from the strips, cut
   90—5×9" rectangles.

2. From each fabric for large half-square triangles, cut
   1—8" strip; from the strip, cut
   16—8×15" rectangles.

3. For the accent borders, cut
   cut 7—1-1/2" strips from red and
   cut 7—2-1/2" strips from gold; sew each set of strips together end to end for two continuous lengths.

4. From fabric for binding, cut
   8—2-1/2" strips; sew the strips end to end for a continuous length.

Sew small and large half-square triangle units

Note: Make 336 small half-square triangles; use 240 to make Four-Patch blocks and 96 to piece the outer border. Make 60—6-1/2" square large half-square triangles.

1. On the wrong side of 45 light 5×9" rectangles, use a sharp fabric pencil or fine-point fabric pen to draw 2—4" square grids. Diagonally draw a line across each square.

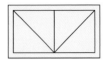

2. Place the gridded rectangles, right sides facing, on dark rectangles, matching raw edges. Sew 1/4" from each diagonal line.

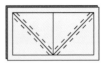

3. Cut along the drawn lines. Each rectangle makes 4 half-square triangles. Press seams toward the darker fabric.

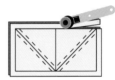

4. Trim each unit to 3-1/2" square, making sure seams are at the corners. Sort the units by color.

5. Use four same-color half-square triangles to make 60 Four-Patch blocks.

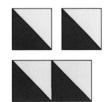

6. With the 8×15" rectangles, proceed as in Steps 1—3, *page 19*, except draw 2—7" grids. Trim the 60 half-square triangles to 6-1/2".

Assemble the rows

1. Lay out the blocks in 12 rows, alternating large half-square triangles with Four-Patch half-square triangles, noting triangle positions.

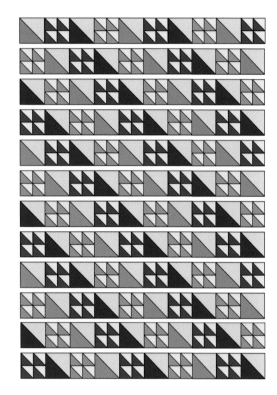

2. Sew each row together. Press seams in one direction, alternating direction for each row. Join the rows, butting block seams for a flat finish.

Sew on the borders

1. Measure the quilt through the center to determine length and width. From length for red accent border, cut two lengths (72-1/2") for the sides and two for the top and bottom (61-1/2"). Sew on the sides; press seams toward the border. Sew on the top and bottom; press seams toward the border.

2. Cut and sew on the 1-1/2×73-1/2" gold side accent border then the 1-1/2×63-1/2" top and bottom borders. Press the seams toward the narrow border.

3. Piece 2 strips of 25 half-square triangles each (75-1/2") and 2 strips of 23 half-square triangles each (69-1/2"). Press seams in one direction. Adjust lengths to fit the quilt.

4. Sew long pieced borders to each side of the quilt. Press toward the gold border. Sew remaining pieced borders to the top and bottom. Press.

5. Sew 1/8" close to the quilt edge.

Row and Border Assembly

Finish the quilt

Refer to General Instructions, *pages 9—15*, to layer, baste, quilt, and bind the quilt.

Cape Cod Finished Quilt Assembly

Cobblestone

Hopscotch through a patio garden along a mossy brick path. The soft, cool shades
and the structured pattern in this quilt are refreshing and inspiring.

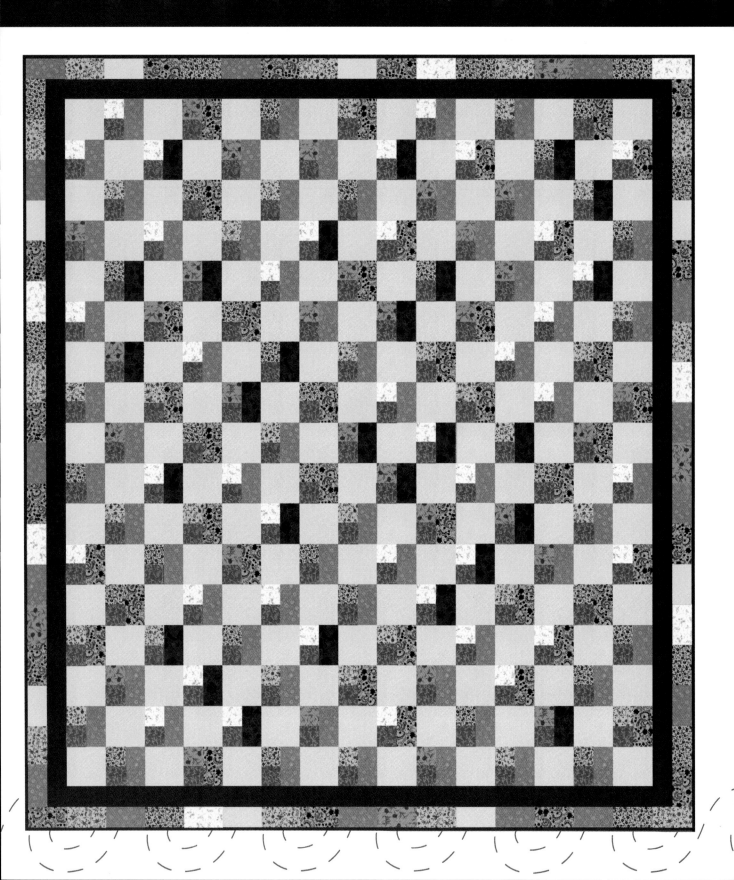

Finished size 68×76"

Select the fabric

*2-1/2 yards light print
or solid for background*

*1 yard assorted light fabric
for blocks and outer border*

*1-3/4 yards assorted medium fabric
for blocks and outer border*

1 yard assorted dark fabric for blocks

*1-1/4 yards dark print or solid fabric for
inner accent border and binding*

4 yards for backing

Cut the fabric

1. From light for background, cut
   16—4-1/2" strips. From 2 of the strips
   cut 9—4-1/2" squares.

2. From light for blocks and border, cut
   8—2-1/2" strips.

3. From medium, cut
   15—2-1/2" strips. From 1 strip cut
   8—4-1/2" rectangles.

4. From dark for blocks, cut
   8—2-1/2" strips.

5. From assorted light and medium, cut
   70—2-1/2×4-1/2" rectangles for the
   outer border.

6. From dark for accent and binding, cut
   14—2-1/2" strips. Sew two sets of
   7 strips end to end for continuous
   lengths. Use one length for an accent
   border and the second for binding.

Sew the block units

1. Right sides together and matching
   long edges, sew together one light and
   one dark 2-1/2" strip to make 8 strip
   sets. Press seams toward the dark
   fabric. From the strip sets, cut 127—2
   1/2" segments for Unit A.

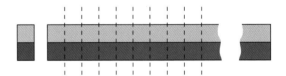

2. Right sides together and matching
   long edges, sew together one 4-1/2"
   background strip and one 2-1/2"
   medium strip to make 14 strip sets.
   Press seams toward the medium fabric.
   From the strip sets, cut 119—4-1/2"
   segments for Unit B.

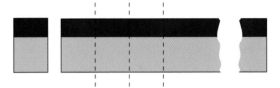

3. Sew a 4-1/2" background
   square to a Unit A to make
   9 of Unit C. Press seams
   toward background fabric.

4. Sew a 2-1/2×4-1/2" medium
   rectangle to a Unit A to make
   8 of Unit D. Press seams
   toward rectangle.

Assemble the rows

1. Lay out units to assemble Row A,
   using 1 Unit C, 7 of Unit B, and 6 of
   Unit A. Sew the units together. Repeat

to make 9 of Row A. Press seams in one direction.

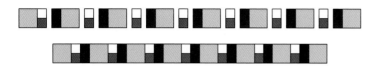

2. Lay out units to assemble Row B, using 7 of Unit A, 7 of Unit B, and 1 Unit D. Sew the units together. Repeat to make 8 of Row B. Press seams in the opposite direction from Row A.

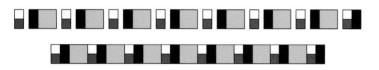

3. Lay out and join the rows, beginning and ending with Row A, alternating with Row B. Press seams in one direction. Stitch close to the edge of the quilt top to reinforce.

Sew on the borders

1. Measure the quilt top lengthwise and widthwise through the center to determine border lengths. From the continuous length for accent border, cut 2—68-1/2" lengths to fit the sides and 2—63-1/2" lengths to fit the top and bottom. Sew on the side borders; press seams toward the border. Sew on the top and bottom borders; press toward the borders.

2. Piece the outer borders. Sew together 18—2-1/2×4-1/2" rectangles to make a border for each side and 17—2-1/2×4-1/2" rectangles to make top and bottom borders. Press seams in one direction. Sew a 72-1/2" border to each side; press seams toward accent borders. Sew on the 68-1/2" top and bottom borders; press seams toward accent borders.

Finish the quilt

Refer to General Instructions, *pages 9–15*, to layer, baste, quilt, and bind the quilt.

Cobblestone Finished Quilt Assembly

Courtyard

Create the illusion of depth and shadow by framing Nine-Patch windows with dark contrasting fabrics. Unite the windows with garden-print sashing and borders.

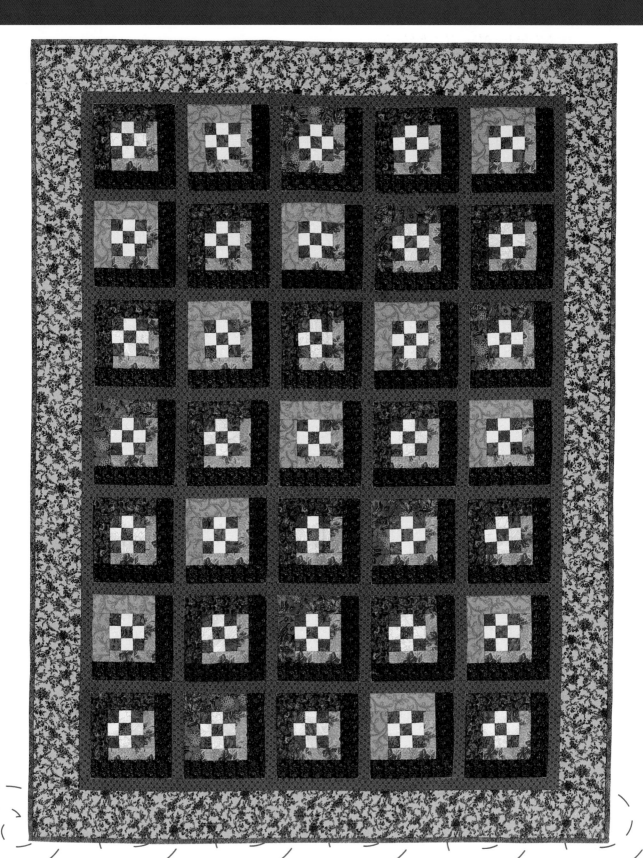

Finished size 49×65"
Finished blocks 8" square

Select the fabric

3/8 yard light for Nine-Patch blocks

1/2 yard dark for Nine-Patch blocks

1/2 yard of medium for Log Cabin block #1 and #2 rectangles

3/4 yard of a second medium for Log Cabin block #3 and #4 rectangles

7/8 yard dark for Log Cabin block #5 and #6 rectangles

1-3/4 yards of a second dark for Log Cabin block #7 and #8 rectangles, inner border, and binding

1 yard complementary fabric for outer border

3 yards backing

Cut the fabric

1. From light, cut
   7—1-1/2" strips.

2. From dark, cut
   8—1-1/2" strips.

3. From medium, cut
   9—1-1/2" strips; from the strips, cut
   35—3-1/2" and 35—4-1/2" rectangles.

4. From a second medium, cut
   11—2" strips; from the strips, cut
   35—4-1/2" and 35—6" rectangles.

5. From dark, cut
   13—2" strips; from the strips, cut
   35—6" and 35—7-1/2" rectangles.

6. From a second dark, cut 7—2-1/2" strips for binding; sew the strips together for a continuous length. 19—1-1/2" strips; from the strips, cut 35—7-1/2" and 35—8-1/2" rectangles. (Use the remaining 1-1/2" strips for inner borders.)

7. From complementary fabric, cut 7—4-1/2" strips for the outer border.

Sew 35 Nine-Patch blocks

1. Make 3 dark-light-dark strip sets, sewing long edges of the 1-1/2" strips together. Press seams toward the dark strip. From the strip sets, cut 70—1-1/2" segments.

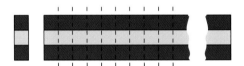

2. Make 2 light-dark-light strip sets. Press seams toward the dark strips. From the strip sets, cut 35—1-1/2" segments.

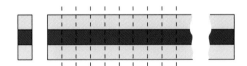

3. Sew together 2 dark-light-dark segments and 1 light-dark-light segment. Repeat to make 35 Nine-Patch blocks.

Sew Log Cabin strips to the Nine-Patch blocks

1. Layout the Nine-Patch blocks and the Log Cabin strips.

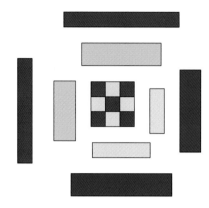

2. Sew a medium 3-1/2" rectangle to the right side of each Nine-Patch, using the chain-piecing method (see General Instructions, *page 13*) to sew the rectangles to the blocks. Press seams toward the Log Cabin strips.

3. Sew a medium 4-1/2" rectangle to the bottom of each Nine-Patch block. Press seams toward the strips.

4. Sew progressively longer rectangles clockwise around the block, ending with the second dark rectangle at the top of each block. Press at each step.

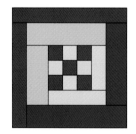

Assemble rows and borders

1. Sew together 7 rows of 5 blocks each, positioning the last narrow dark strip sewn to each block at the top of each row.

2. Sew the rows together; press seams in one direction.

3. Measure lengthwise through the center of the quilt. Cut and sew the 1-1/2" dark strip to the right side.

4. Measure the quilt top lengthwise through the center. From the outer border length cut two strips to size and sew one to each side of the quilt. Press seams toward the borders.

5. Measure the quilt top widthwise through the center. From the outer border length cut two strips to size and sew one to the top and one to the bottom of the quilt. Press.

Finish the quilt

Refer to General Instructions, *pages 9–15*, to layer, baste, quilt, and bind the quilt.

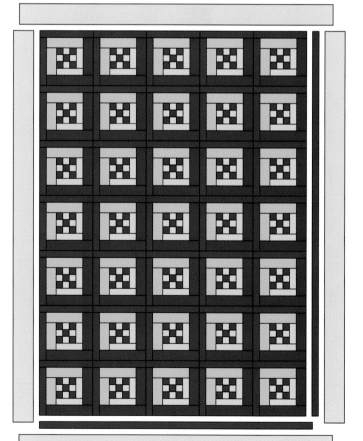

Row and Border Assembly

Courtyard Finished Quilt Assembly

English Garden

Prim and proper posies are neatly aligned in this cozy, vintage-looking quilt. Select fabrics that imitate your favorite blooms to make a garden full of color.

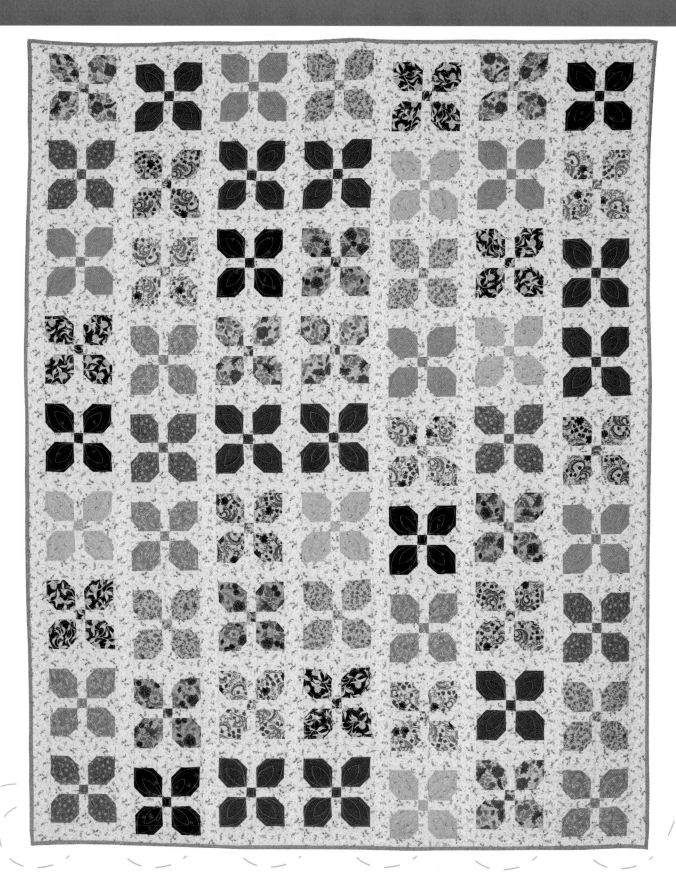

Finished size 65×82"
63 blocks, 5 of each color, finished size 7" square

Select the fabric

13 assorted fat-quarter prints (18×22")

4-1/2 yards background fabric

2/3 yard binding

4 yards backing

Cut the fabric

1. From each fat-quarter, cut
   5—3-1/2" strips and 1—1-1/2" strip.
   From each 3-1/2" strip, cut
   4—3-1/2" squares (252 total) Separate
   the colors in stacks of four.

2. From background fabric, cut
   18—1-1/2" strips; from the strips, cut
   504—1-1/2" squares.

   16—2-1/2" strips; sew the strips
   together end to end in sets of two, cut
   8—82-1/2" strips.

   5—3-1/2" strips; from the strips, cut
   126—1-1/2×3-1/2" rectangles.

   5—7-1/2" strips; from the strips, cut
   63—2-1/2×7-1/2" rectangles and
   7—1-1/2×7-1/2" rectangles.

   7—3-1/2" strips; from the strips, cut
   26—3-1/2×10" rectangles.

Sew 63 Flower Blocks

1. Use template-free angle-piecing to
   make the flower units.
   Right sides together, lay
   a 1-1/2" background
   square along opposite

corners of a 3-1/2" print
square. Draw a diagonal
pencil line across the two
outer corners of each small
square. Sew on the lines.
Trim the seam to 1/4";
press the background
triangle to outer edge.

2. Make 13 strip sets for the flower
   centers by sewing a 3-1/2×10"
   background strip to both long edges
   of a 1-1/2" print strip. Press seams
   away from the center. From each strip
   set, cut 5—1-1/2×10" flower center
   units. Separate by color.

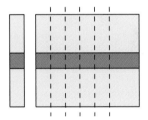

3. Sew same color flower units to each
   long side of a 1-1/2×3-1/2"
   background strip to make 126 units.
   Press seams toward the center.

4. Match and sew flower center units to
   two flower units, noting direction of
   flower petals. Press the blocks.

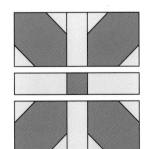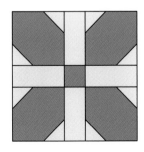

Assemble the quilt top

1. Lay out the blocks for color arrangement in 7 vertical rows of 9 blocks each.

2. Lay out the short background sashing strips with the blocks, using 9—7-1/2×2-1/2" and 1—7-1/2×1-1/2" for each row, alternating the 1-1/2" strip from the bottom to the top of adjacent rows. Sew the sashing to the blocks to join the blocks in rows. Press seams toward the sashing.

3. Sew the 2-1/2×82-1/2" background strips between the vertical rows and to each long side. Press seams toward the background strip.

Finish the quilt

Refer to General Instructions, *pages 9–15,* to layer, baste, quilt, and bind the quilt.

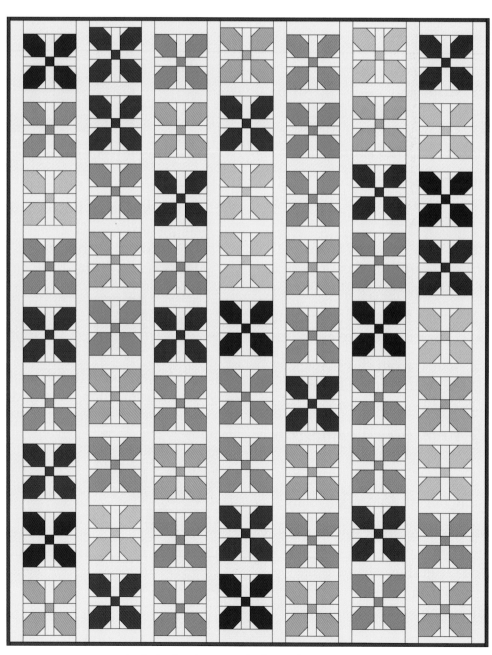

English Garden Finished Quilt Assembly

English Garden Quilting Designs

Garden Wall

Imagine ivy twining along a shady garden wall with dappled sunlight peeping through. Recreate this refreshing vision with assorted garden prints.

Finished size 45×64-1/2"
Finished block 4-1/2" square

Select the fabric

1-1/4 yards dark for center squares,
inner border, and binding

14 assorted medium fat-quarters (18×22")

14 assorted light fat-quarters

4-1/4 yards for backing

Cut the fabric

Note: The blocks, which consist of a medium and light side, are reversed during construction. For Block A, cut rectangles #2 and #3 from darker fabric than rectangles #4 and #5; for Block B, cut rectangles #2 and #3 from lighter fabric than rectangles #4 and #5.

1. From dark, cut
   4—2" strips; from the strips cut
   94—2" center squares; label them #1.

   6—3-1/2" strips; sew the strips end to end for a continuous length to cut to size for inner borders.

   6—2-1/2" strips; sew the strips end to end for continuous binding length.

2. Layer 4 fat-quarters; trim the edges even. From each layer cut 4—2" strips. From the strips, cut and label 94 each:
   #2—2" square
   #3—3-1/2" rectangle
   #4—3-1/2" rectangle
   #5—5" rectangle

3. From assorted fat-quarters, cut
   2—4-1/4" squares; cut each square in half diagonally for 4 corner triangles.

6—7-3/4" squares; cut each square in half diagonally twice (in an X) for 24 setting triangles.

From remaining fat-quarter fabric, cut 2"-wide rectangles at various lengths to use to piece the border.

Sew 54 of Block A

1. Sew a #1 dark center square and a medium #2 square together. Press.

2. Rotating clockwise, use the same fabric as #2 and sew a #3 rectangle to the unit.

3. Sew a light #4 rectangle clockwise from the #3 rectangle.

4. Sew a same fabric #5 rectangle to the unit. Press seams toward the edge of the block.

Sew 40 of Block B

1. Sew a #1 dark center square and a light #2 square together. Press.

2. Rotating clockwise, use the same fabric as #2 and sew a #3 rectangle to the unit.

3. Sew a medium #4 rectangle clockwise from the #3 rectangle.

4. Sew a same fabric #5 rectangle to the unit. Press seams toward the edge of the block.

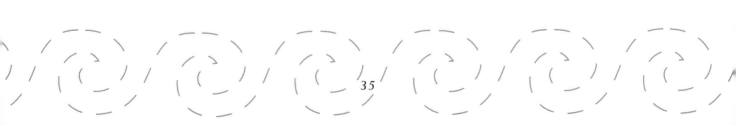

Assemble the rows

1. Use the illustrations *below* as a guide to lay out blocks for color placement.

2. Sew rows together with the setting and corner triangles.

3. Align a ruler along the outer edge; mark and trim the edges even, leaving 1/4" seam allowance all around. Stabilize the quilt top with a row of stitches close to the outer edge.

Sew on the borders

1. Measure the quilt top lengthwise through the center. From the continuous dark length, cut two strips to size and sew one to each side of the quilt. Press seams toward the borders.

2. Measure the quilt top widthwise through the center. Cut two dark inner border strips and sew one to the top and one to the bottom of the quilt. Press seams toward the borders.

3. To make the outer scrappy border, piece the 2"-wide strips end to end. Measure as for Steps 1 and 2 *above* and sew side borders, then top and bottom borders to the quilt top. Press seams toward the inner borders.

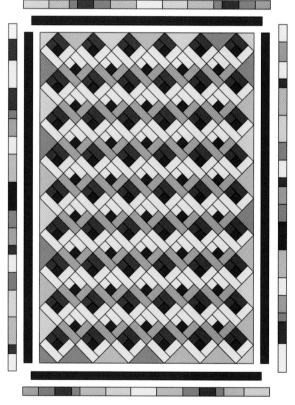

Row and Border Assembly

Finish the quilt

Refer to General Instructions, *pages 9–15,* to layer, baste, quilt, and bind the quilt.

Garden Wall Finished Quilt Assembly

Gramma Lera's Garden

Reminiscent of vintage Grandmother's Flower Garden quilts, yet much easier,
these fabric blooms appear to border an old-fashioned picket fence.

Finished size 58-1/2×72-1/2"

42 blocks 5-1/2×9-1/2"

Select the fabric

2/3 yard each of 5 assorted lights
for background

7/8 yard light for sashing
(Optional: 3-1/8 yards of one light
for background and sashing)

1/6 yard each of 7 or
more colorful prints for flowers

1/4 yard total of assorted scraps
for flower centers
(Optional: 1/4 yard of one fabric)

1/2 yard green for leaves and stems

1 yard bright yellow for
inner border and binding

1 yard blue print for outer border

2 yards lightweight fusible adhesive

Template plastic

Contrasting Perlé cotton

Cut the fabric

1. From each assorted light for
    background, cut 7 strips to measure:
    1-3/4", 2-1/4", 2-1/2", 3", and 3-1/2"
    (Optional: Cut 42—6-1/2×11"
    rectangles.)

2. From light for sashing, cut
    15—1-3/4" strips. Sew the strips end
    to end for a continuous length; from
    the strips, cut
    8—60-1/2" lengths and
    2—49" lengths.

3. From assorted prints for flowers, cut
    42—5-1/2" squares.

4. From fabric for flower centers,
    cut 42—2-1/2" squares. (Optional:
    Leave the 1/4 yard intact.)

5. From bright yellow, cut
    7—1-1/2" strips for inner border
    7—2-1/2" strips for binding. (Sew
    each set of strips together for two
    continuous lengths.)

6. From blue print, cut
    7—4-1/2" strips for the outer border.
    Join the strips after measuring the
    length and width of the quilt top; then
    cut them to size.

Piece block backgrounds

1. Sew together 7 strip sets (if not using
    the optional solid background) in this
    order from top to bottom: 3-1/2",
    2-1/2", 3", 1-3/4", and 2-1/4". Press the
    seams in one direction.

2. From the strip sets, cut 42—6 1/2"
    background rectangles.

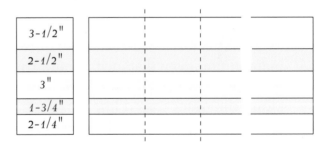

Trace, cut, and fuse the flowers

1. Trace Templates A—F, *page 42,* onto
    template plastic; cut out shapes with
    sharp scissors.

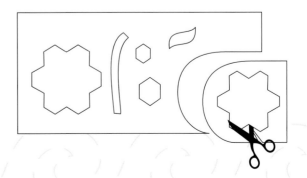

2. Trace 42 of Template A and 42 of Template B to fusible adhesive; cut the shapes on the lines.

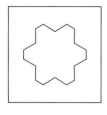 

3. Center and fuse the fusible adhesive flowers to the wrong side of each 5-1/2" square, leaving the paper intact.

4. Center and trace the larger flower (Template C) over the adhesive fused to the fabric square, maintaining even distance around the petals. Cut out the flower along the outer traced line.

5. Fuse the flower centers to the wrong side of the 2-1/2" squares, leaving the paper intact. (Optional: Fuse flower centers to wrong side of 1/4 yard fabric, allowing approximately 3/4" between each shape). Center and trace the larger flower center (Template D) over the adhesive fused to the fabric, maintaining even distance around the edges. Cut out the flower centers along the outer traced line.

6. Fuse adhesive to green fabric. Trace Templates E and F on the paper side of the adhesive. Cut out shapes on the traced lines.

7. Position flowers 1" from the top of each 6-1/2" background rectangle; position flower centers. Place stem under the base of each flower, alternating stem directions. Position a leaf on each side of the stems. Fuse the fabric to the

background, following adhesive manufacturer's directions.

8. Use Perlé cotton to stitch around the flowers, centers, stems, and leaves 1/8" from the edges and between the flower petals. Use a needle to fray the fabric edges; trim the edges.

9. Trim blocks to measure 6×10-1/2".

Assemble rows and sashing

1. Lay out blocks in 7 rows of 6 blocks each, stems in alternate directions. Sew each row. Press seams toward stem ends.

2. Join the rows together with 1-3/4×60-1/2" sashing strips. Sew 1-3/4" strips to the sides then to the top and bottom. Press seams toward sashing.

Sew on borders

1. Measure the length and width of the quilt. Cut and sew inner border to the sides, then to the top and bottom. Press.

2. Cut and sew the outer borders to the sides, then top and bottom. Press.

3. Use a needle to fray the edges of the flower center and the flower petals.

Finish the quilt

Refer to General Instructions, *pages 9–15*, to layer, baste, quilt, and bind the quilt.

Gramma Lera's Garden Finished Quilt Assembly

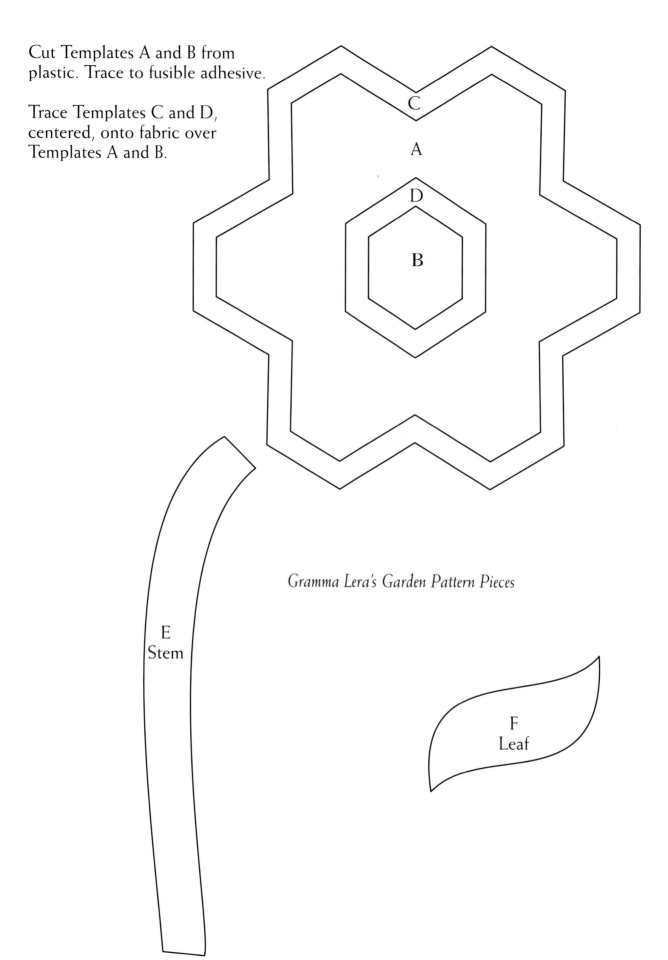

Cut Templates A and B from plastic. Trace to fusible adhesive.

Trace Templates C and D, centered, onto fabric over Templates A and B.

C

A

D

B

E
Stem

Gramma Lera's Garden Pattern Pieces

F
Leaf

Gramma Lera's Garden
Free-Motion Quilting Designs

A-tisket, A-tasket

Use bright fabrics to "weave" a summery quilt basket to use at picnics, on lawn furniture, or to lay across a wicker chair for decor that's as fresh as crisp apples.

Finished size 56-1/2×56-1/2"
Finished Nine-Patch blocks 3-3/4" square
Finished Rail blocks 2-1/2×3-3/4"

Select the fabric

1-1/8 yards dark red

1 yard medium red

1-1/8 yards dark green

1 yard medium green

1-1/2 yards light print for background

3-1/4 yards for backing

5/8 yard red for binding

Cut the fabric

1. From dark red, cut
   21—1-3/4" strips.

2. From medium red, cut
   16—1-3/4" strips.

3. From dark green, cut
   14—1-3/4" strips.

4. From medium green, cut
   19—1-3/4" strips.

5. From light print, cut
   17—1-3/4" strips; from 3 strips, cut
   32—1-3/4 x 3" rectangles and
   4—1-3/4" squares

   5—3" strips; from the strips, cut
   64—3" squares.

6. From red, cut
   6—2-1/2" strips. Sew the strips end to
   end for a continuous binding length.

Sew 81 Nine-Patch blocks

1. For Nine-Patch Block A, sew a dark
   red strip to both sides of a medium
   green strip. Make 3 dark red-medium
   green-dark red strip sets. Press seams
   toward the red fabric. From the strip
   sets, cut 50—1-3/4" segments.

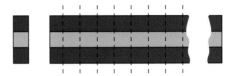

Sew a medium green strips to both
sides of a dark red strip. Press seams
toward the red fabric. From the strip
sets, cut 25—1-3/4" segments.

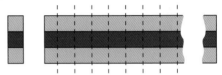

2. Sew a red-green-red segment to each
   long side of a green-red-green
   segment to complete 25 Nine-Patch
   Block A. Press seams toward the block
   edges. The unfinished blocks should
   measure 4-1/2" square.

3. For Nine-Patch Block B, sew 2 dark
   red-dark green-dark red strip sets.
   Press seams toward red fabric. From
   strip sets, cut 40—1-3/4" segments.

   Sew a dark green-dark red-dark green
   strip set, press seams toward red fabric,
   and cut 20—1-3/4" segments.

   Sew a red-green-red segment to each
   green-red-green segment to complete
   20 Nine-Patch Block B units. Press
   seams toward the block edges.

4. For Nine-Patch Block C, sew 2 medium red-medium green-medium red strip sets. Press seams toward red fabric and cut 40—1-3/4" segments.

Sew a medium green-medium red-medium green strip set, press seams to red fabric; cut 20—1-3/4" segments.

Sew a red-green-red segment to each side of a green-red-green segment to complete 20 Nine-Patch Block C units. Press seams toward block edges.

5. For Nine-Patch Block D, sew 2 medium red-dark green-medium red strips sets. Press seams toward red fabric; cut 32—1-3/4" segments.

Sew a dark green-medium red-dark green strip set, press seams toward red fabric; cut 16—1-3/4" segments.

Sew a red-green-red segment to each side of a green-red-green segment to complete 16 Nine-Patch Block D units. Press seams toward block edges.

Sew the Rail blocks

1. For Rail block units E and F, sew 4 strip sets from dark red-light print-dark red. Press seams toward the light print. From the strip sets, cut 40—3" segments and 10—1-3/4" segments.

2. For Rail block units G and H, sew 3 strip sets from medium red-light print-medium red. Press seams toward light print. From strip sets, cut 32—3" segments and 8—1-3/4" segments.

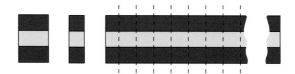

3. For Rail block units I and J, sew 3 strip sets from dark green-light print-dark green. Press seams toward the light print. From the strip sets, cut 32—3" segments and 8—1-3/4" segments.

4. For Rail block units K and L, sew 4 strip sets from medium green-light print-medium green. Press seams toward light print. From the strip sets, cut 40—3" and 10—1-3/4" segments.

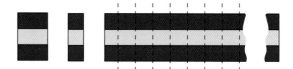

Assemble the rows

1. Using the illustration, *below*, join the blocks to make the following rows: 2 of Row A, 5 of Row B, 8 of Row C, and 4 of Row D.

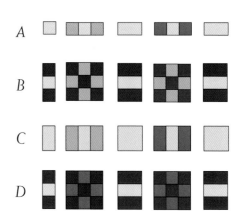

2. Lay out and join the rows, beginning and ending with Row A, alternating Row C between Rows B and D.

3. Press the quilt top. Stitch 1/8" close to the edges all around.

Finish the quilt

Refer to General Instructions, *pages 9–15*, to layer, baste, quilt, and bind the quilt.

A-Tisket, A Tasket Finished Quilt Assembly

American Colonial

Celebrate Independence Day by making a quilt that resembles patriotic buntings.
Embellished with red and blue buttons, it's sure to be a holiday centerpiece.

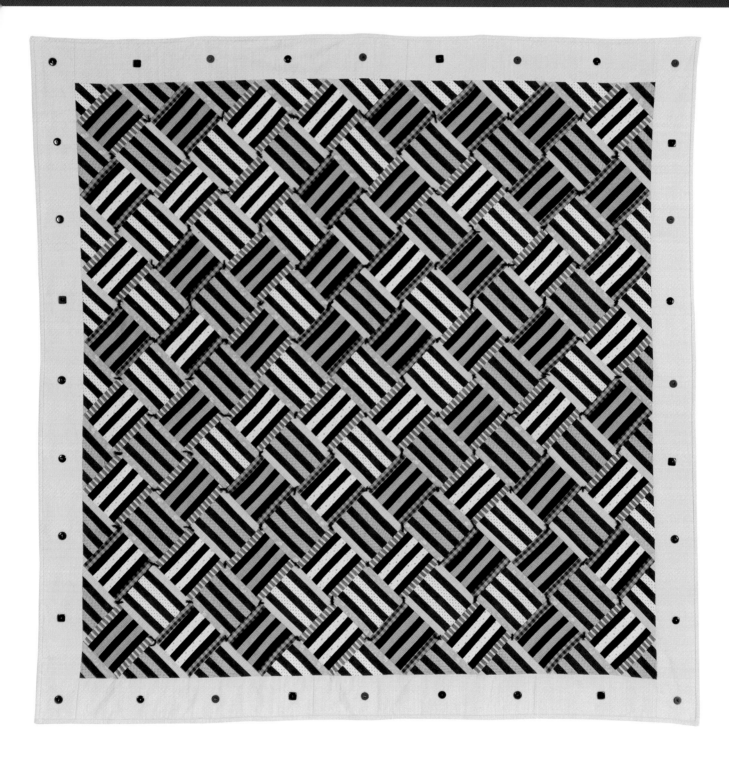

Finished size 66" square

Select the fabric

1-1/2 yards solid blue

1-1/2 yards solid red

1/2 yard each light blue, medium blue,
light blue plaid, and medium blue stripe

1/2 yard each light red, medium red,
light red plaid, and medium red stripe

1-1/2 yards white

2 yards backing

32 assorted red and blue buttons

Cut the fabric

1. From each solid blue and red, cut
    36—1-1/4" strips.

2. From each assorted blue and red, cut
    12—1-1/4" strips.

3. From white, cut
    6—4-1/4" strips for borders and
    6—2-1/2" strips for binding.
    Sew each set of strips together for
    continuous lengths. Cut the borders to
    fit after measuring the quilt top.

Sew strip sets and
cut segments

1. Sew 6 blue strip sets using 3 solid
    blue, 2 light blue plaid, and 2 medium
    blue strips for each. Press seams in one
    direction. The width of the strip set
    should measure 5-3/4". From each

strip, cut 7—5-3/4" segments, for
42 units. (All segments must be the
same size square.)

2. Sew 6 blue strip sets using 3 solid
    blue, 2 light blue, and 2 medium blue
    stripe strips for each. Press seams in
    one direction. Cut 7—5-3/4" segments
    from each strip set, for 42 units.

3. Sew 6 red strip sets using 3 solid red,
    2 light red, and 2 medium red stripe
    strips for each. Press seams in one
    direction. Cut 7—5-3/4" segments
    from each strip set, for 42 units.

4. Sew 6 red strip sets using 3 solid red,
    2 medium red, and 2 light red plaid
    strips for each. Press seams in one
    direction. Cut 7—5-3/4" segments
    from each strip set, for 42 units.

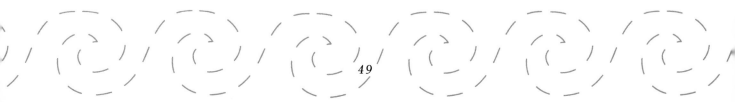

Assemble the quilt top

1. Lay out rows alternating red and blue units. The first row is a single unit; add two units to each row until the ninth row (17 units); then deduct two units for each row to end with a single unit.

2. Join the units to make each row. Press seams in one direction, press seams of adjacent rows in alternate directions.

3. Sew together the rows, butting block seam allowances for a flat finish and matching raw edges of shorter rows seam allowance of units in longer rows. Press the seams flat.

4. Lay the quilt top flat. Along the outer edge of the quilt top, measure 1/8" away from points of the blue blocks (toward the edge of the quilt) and use a ruler and rotary cutter or a straightedge, pencil, and scissors to mark and evenly trim along the edges of the quilt top. Stitch 1/4" from the from the outer edge all around the quilt.

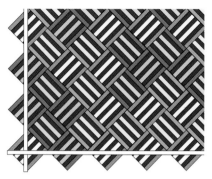

Sew on the borders

1. Measure the quilt lengthwise through the center. Cut two white lengths to fit and sew one to each side of the quilt. Press seams toward the borders.

2. Measure the quilt widthwise through the center. Cut two white lengths to fit; sew to the top and bottom. Press seams toward the borders.

Finish the quilt

1. Refer to General Instructions, *pages 9–15*, to layer, baste, quilt, and bind the quilt.

2. Sew red and blue buttons along the outer border, using the Finished Quilt Assembly diagram for placement.

Row Assembly

American Colonial Finished Quilt Assembly

Blue Pinwheels

Light breezes send vanes of blue spinning across this tone-on-tone quilt, artfully stirring and blending monochromatic hues in energetic movement.

Finished size 52×64"

Select the fabric

1 yard dark blue print

1-3/8 yards medium blue print

1-3/8 yards light blue print

4-3/8 yards off-white print

*9 yards binding
(purchased or made from 2-1/2" strips)*

4 yards backing

Cut the fabric

1. From dark blue print, cut 7—2-7/8" strips; from the strips cut 92—2-7/8" squares.

2. From medium blue print, cut 8—2-7/8" strips; from the strips cut 108—2-7/8" squares.

3. From light blue print, cut 9—2-7/8" strips; from the strips cut 124—2-7/8" squares.

4. From off-white print, cut 24—2-7/8" strips; from the strips cut 324—2-7/8" squares.

   7—4-1/2" strips; sew the strips end to end for a continuous length.

Sew 162 Pinwheel blocks

1. Draw a diagonal line corner to corner on each off-white 2-7/8" square with a sharp pencil.

2. Match an off-white square to each blue square, right sides together. Sew 1/4" from each side of the diagonal line. Press the units flat. Cut on the pencil line. Press seams toward the blue triangle.

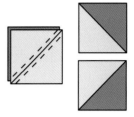

3. Using same color combinations, join half-square triangles in units of 2, noting placement. Press seams toward blue triangle. Join 2 units to make each Pinwheel block; press.

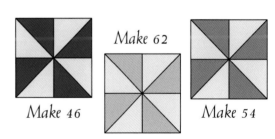

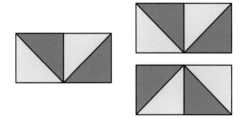

Make 62

Make 46

Make 54

Assemble the rows and borders

1. Layout Pinwheel blocks for quilt center in 12 horizontal rows of 9 blocks each, referring to Row and Border Assembly, *page 54.*

2. Sew rows of Pinwheel blocks together. Press the seams in one direction for each row, alternating directions for adjacent rows.

3. Join the rows, matching seams for a smooth finish. Press long seams flat.

4. From the 4-1/2" off-white length, cut 2—48-1/2" and 2—44-1/2" strips. Sew a long strip to each side of the quilt top. Press seams toward the inner border. Sew short strips to the top and bottom of the quilt top. Press the seams toward the inner order.

5. Noting color placement, lay out and join 2 rows of 14 Pinwheel blocks each for each long side of the quilt. Sew a row to each side; press the seams toward the inner border.

6. Lay out and join 2 rows of 13 Pinwheel blocks each for the top and bottom of the quilt. Sew a row to the top and bottom; press the seams toward the inner border.

7. Sew a basting stitch 1/8" from the edge of the quilt top to stabilize for layering and binding.

Finish the quilt

Refer to General Instructions, *pages 9–15*, to layer, baste, quilt, and bind the quilt.

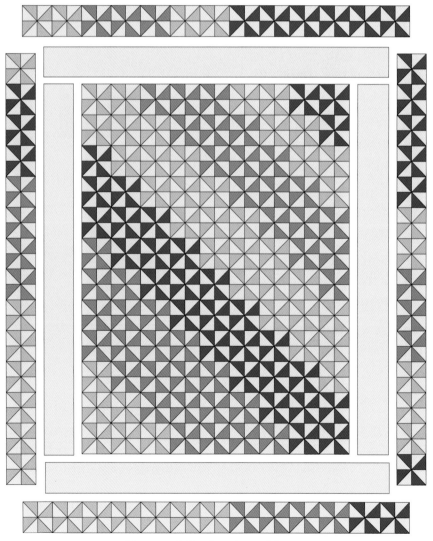

Row and Border Assembly

Blue Pinwheels Finished Quilt Assembly

Blue Pinwheels Quilting Design

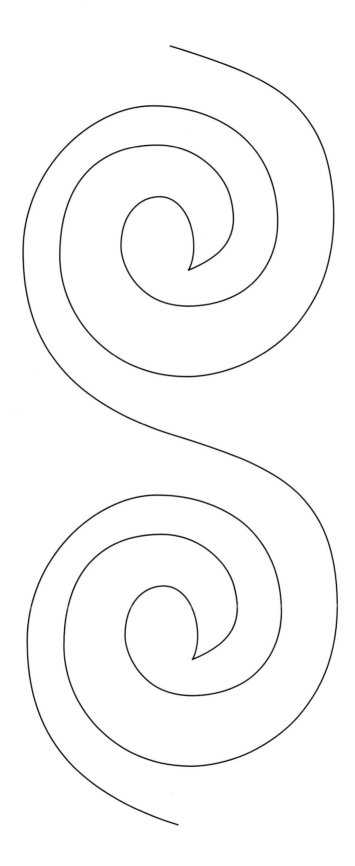

Blue Pinwheels Quilting Design

Count Your Blessings

Baa, Baa, cuddly Log Cabin Sheep!
Will your warm woven plaids keep us cozy through the night?

Finished quilt 57×68"
Finished Lamb blocks 9×13"

Select the fabric

1/3 yard each of 15 assorted fabrics
for blocks and borders

1 yard red print or solid for sashing

1/4 yard small check for corner stones

1 yard dotted black for accent border
and binding

3-1/2 yards for backing

3/8 yard each black wool and red wool
for appliqué

1-1/8 yards lightweight fusible adhesive

Embroidery floss to match wool

Cut the fabric

1. From each assorted fabric, cut
   10—1-1/2×22" strips.

   From strips, cut
   75—3-1/2" Log Cabin rectangles for
   positions #1, #2, #3, #4, and #5.

   60—5-1/2" Log Cabin rectangles for
   positions #6, #7, #8, and #9.

   60—7-1/2" Log Cabin rectangles for
   positions #10, #11, #12, and #13.

   90—9-1/2" Log Cabin rectangles for
   positions #14, #15, #16, #17, #18,
   and #19.

2. From red for sashing, cut
   18—3×13-1/2" rectangles and
   20—3×9-1/2" rectangles.

3. From check for corner stones, cut
   24—3" squares.

4. From dotted black, cut
   6—1-1/2" strips; sew the strips end to

end for a continuous length for the
accent border.

7—2-1/2" strips; sew the strips end to
end for continuous binding length.

5. From remaining assorted fabrics, cut
   54—1-1/2×22" strips for the
   checkerboard pieced border.

Sew 15 Lamb blocks

1. Referring to the illustration, *below,* lay
   out the Log Cabin rectangles for each
   block. Join the rectangles in numerical
   order, chain-stitching all #1 and #2
   rectangles before proceeding to the
   next rectangles. Press seams toward
   the last rectangle sewn. After rectangle
   #19 is sewn on and pressed, square the
   block. The block should measure
   9-1/2×13-1/3"; make any necessary
   adjustments before joining blocks.

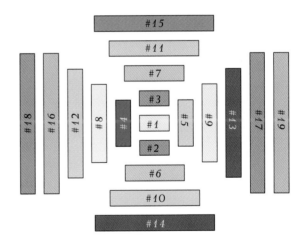

Sew sashing strips and Corner Stones to Lamb blocks

1. Sew together 6 sets of sashing strips using 3—3×13-1/2" sashing rectangles and 4—3" squares. Press the seams toward the rectangles.

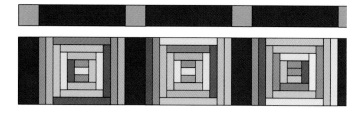

2. Sew a 3×9-1/2" sashing rectangle to one 9-1/2" side of each Lamb Block. To 5 Lamb Blocks, sew a second sashing rectangle to the opposite side. Sew together 5 rows of 3 Lamb Blocks each.

3. Lay out the sashing strips with corner blocks and the Lamb Block rows. Sew the rows together. Press the quilt top.

Sew on the accent border

1. From the 1-1/2" continuous length, cut 2 strips 60-1/2". Sew a length to each side of the quilt top. Cut 51-1/2" lengths for the top and bottom; sew the lengths to the top and bottom; press seams toward the border.

Piece the outer Checkerboard border

1. Sew 3 assorted 1-1/2×22" strips together to make a total of 17 strip sets. Press seams in one direction.

2. From each strip set, cut 14—1-1/2" segments across the strip.

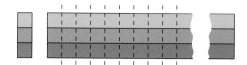

3. Sew segments together to make 2—62-segment (62-1/2") and 2—57-segment strips (57-1/2") for the sides, top, and bottom. Adjust lengths to fit. Sew a pieced border to each side, then the top and bottom. Press seams toward the accent border.

Appliqué the Lamb heads, hearts, and legs

1. Trace and cut out the patterns, *page 63*. Following manufacturer's directions, fuse adhesive to the wool fabrics.

2. From black wool, cut out 15 lamb heads and 60 legs. From red wool, cut 15 hearts.

3. Fuse the wool pieces to the quilt top, using the photograph, *page 58*, and the illustration, *page 62*, as guides.

4. Appliqué the wool pieces to the quilt top using 2 strands of embroidery floss and buttonhole stitches along the edge of each piece.

Finish the quilt

Refer to General Instructions, *pages 9–15*, to layer, baste, quilt, and bind the quilt.

Sashing, Row, and Border Assembly

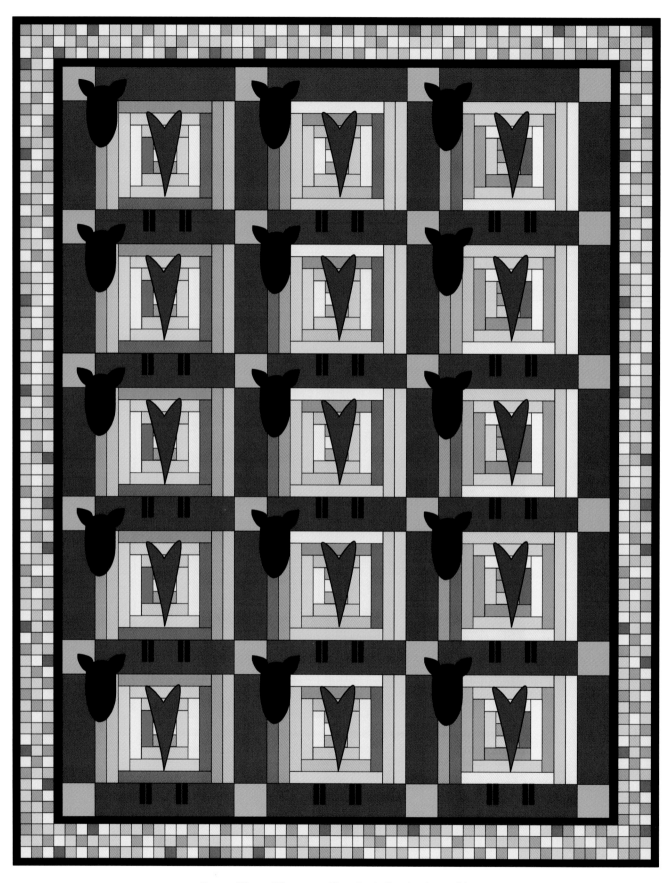

Count Your Blessings Finished Quilt Assembly

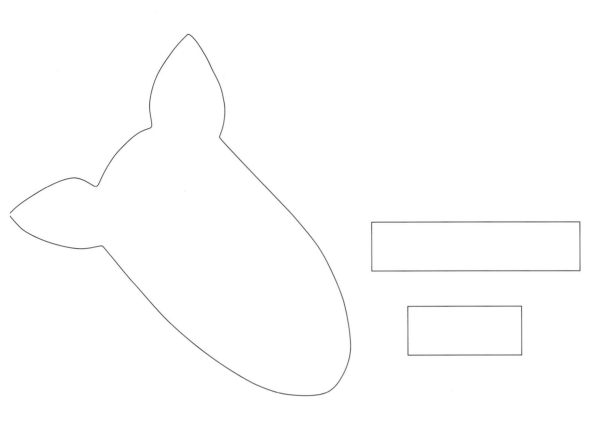

Count Your Blessings Lamb head, legs, and heart patterns

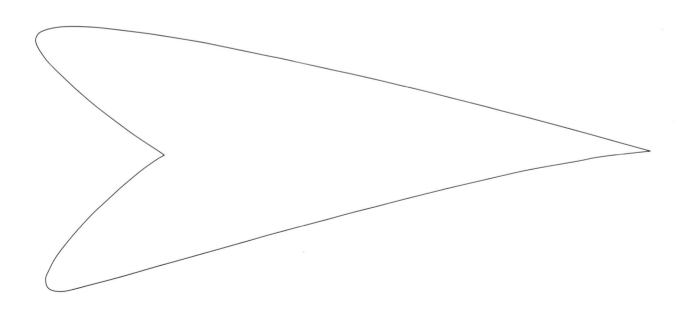

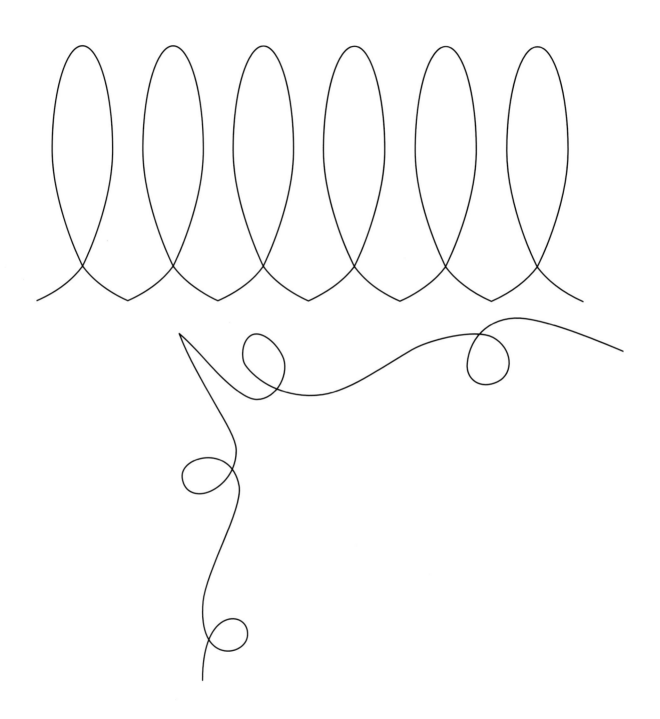

Count Your Blessings Free-Motion Quilting Designs

Count Your Blessings Quilting Designs

Flying Geese Log Cabin

Two distinctively traditional American blocks—pieced from assorted homespun fabrics—recall the maxim: "Use it up, wear it out, make it do, or do without."

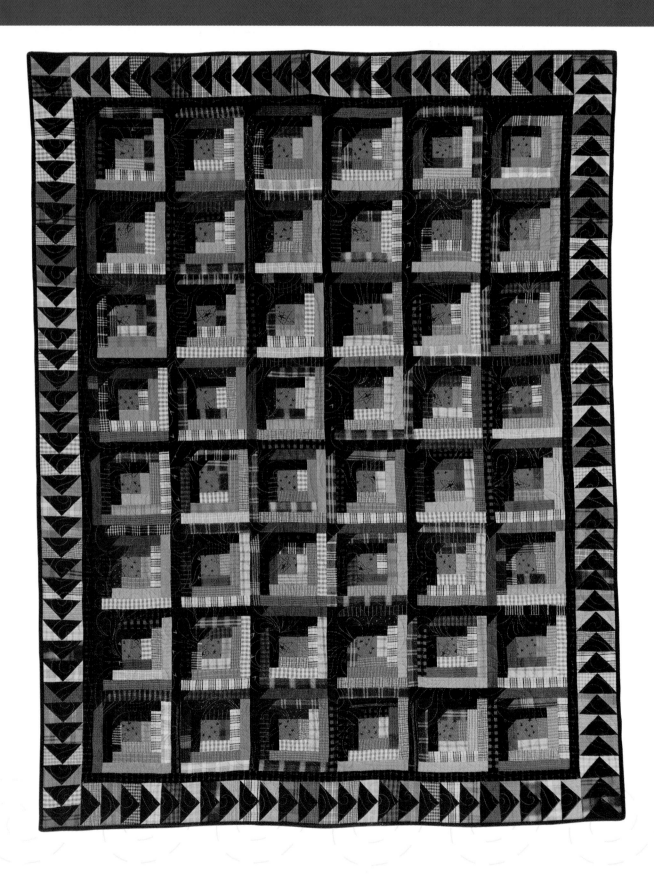

Finished size 58×74"
Finished blocks 8" square

Select the fabric

2-5/8 yards red plaid for
Flying Geese blocks and binding

1/2 yard each of 10 assorted
light prints and plaids

1/3 yard each of 8 assorted
dark prints and plaids

1/3 yard gold for block centers

1/3 yard dark plaid for inner border

4 yards for backing

Cut the fabric

1. From red plaid, cut
9—2-1/2" strips;
from the strips, cut
144—2-1/2" squares
to make Flying
Geese blocks.

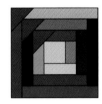

7—4-1/2" strips; from the strips, cut
124—2-1/2×4-1/2" rectangles for the
Flying Geese border.

7—2-1/2" strips; sew the strips end to
end for continuous binding length.

2. From each of the assorted light prints
and plaids, cut 6—1-1/2" strips; from
the strips, cut 48 Log Cabin rectangles
each of the following lengths (label
and sort strips by block position):
#2—2-1/2"; #3—3-1/2"; #6—4-1/2";
#7—5-1/2"; #10—6-1/2"; #11—7-1/2".

Also from assorted light, cut
18—2-1/2" strips; from the strips, cut
248—2-1/2" squares for the Flying
Geese border.

3. From each of the assorted dark prints
and plaids, cut
6—1-1/2" strips; from the strips, cut
48 Log Cabin rectangles each of the
following lengths (label and sort strips
by block position):
#4—3-1/2"; #5—4-1/2"; #8—5-1/2";
#9—6-1/2"; #12—7-1/2"; #13—8-1/2".

4. From gold, cut 48—2-1/2" squares
for block centers; label them #1.

5. From dark plaid, cut 7—1-1/2" strips;
sew them end to end for a continuous
length to use for the inner border.
After piecing the quilt top, measure
and cut the borders to fit (2—64-1/2"
side lengths and 2—50-1/2" top and
bottom lengths).

Sew 48 Flying Geese Log Cabin blocks

1. To one side of a #1 gold
square, sew a #2 Log
Cabin rectangle, using
the chain-piecing
method to join all the #1
and #2 pieces. Press.
Sewing clockwise and pressing after
each step, sew #3, #4, and #5 Log
Cabin rectangles to the unit. The
blocks should measure
4-1/2" square. Adjust the size by
trimming if necessary.

2. For Flying Geese on block
corners, draw a diagonal
line from corner to corner
on the wrong side of each
2-1/2" red plaid square.
Right sides together, lay a
square along the corner of
Log Cabin rectangles #4
and #5. Sew on the line.
Trim the seam to 1/4"; press
the Flying Geese triangle open.

3. Sewing clockwise, sew Log Cabin strips #6 through #9 to the unit. The block should measure 6-1/2" square. Adjust the size by trimming and squaring if necessary. Follow Step 2 to join a Flying Geese triangle to the corner of rectangles #8 and #9.

4. Continuing clockwise, sew Log Cabin rectangles #10 through #13 to the blocks. The block should measure 8-1/2" square; square and trim if necessary. Follow Step 2 to join Flying Geese triangles to Log Cabin rectangles #12 and #13.

Assemble the rows

1. Lay out the blocks, aligning Flying Geese in one direction.

2. Sew the blocks together in 8 rows of 6 blocks each. The quilt top should measure 48-1/2×64-1/2".

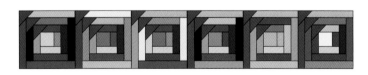

Piece 124 Flying Geese for the border

1. Draw a diagonal line from corner to corner on the 2-1/2" light background squares. Right sides together, sew a 2-1/2" light square to one side of a 2-1/2×4-1/2" red plaid rectangle. Trim

the seam of the light fabric *only* to 1/4". Press the triangle open. Sew a 2-1/2" light background square to the opposite side of the rectangle. Trim the seam and press open.

2. Noting placement, sew together 2 rows each of 33 Flying Geese and 2 rows each of 29 Flying Geese. Press seams in one direction, taking care to avoid stretching or pulling the seams.

Sew on the borders

1. Sew a 64-1/2" dark plaid inner border strip to each side of the quilt top; press. Sew the 50-1/2" strips to the quilt top and bottom; press.

2. Noting direction of Flying Geese in each strip, sew a 33-unit Flying Geese border strip to each long side of the quilt top; press. Sew a 29-unit Flying Geese border strip to the top and the bottom of the quilt; press.

3. Stabilize the quilt top with a 1/8" basting stitch along the raw edges.

Finish the quilt

Refer to General Instructions, *pages 9–15*, to layer, baste, quilt, and bind the quilt.

Flying Geese Log Cabin Finished Quilt Assembly

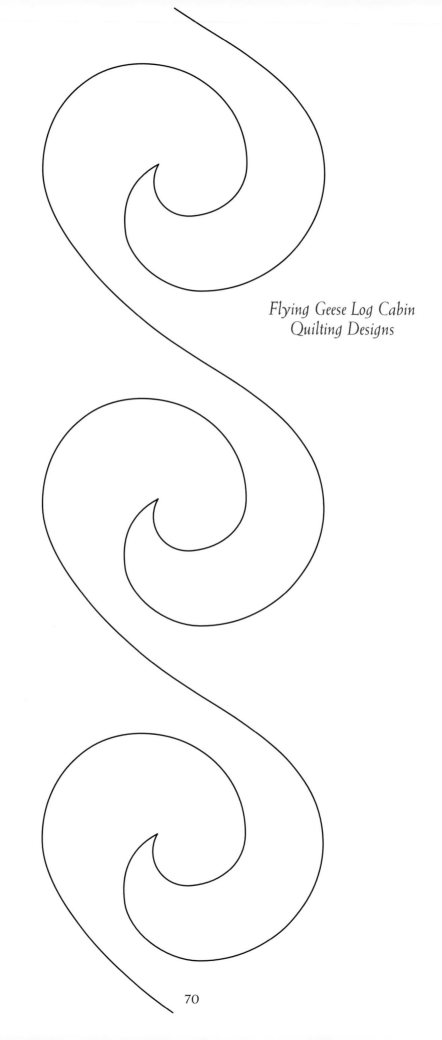

*Flying Geese Log Cabin
Quilting Designs*

70

Flying Geese Log Cabin Quilting Designs

Horizon Sails

Movement that resembles schooners skimming across the sea is achieved with contrasting fabrics and by rotating triangle squares between sunset-color borders.

Finished size 72×80"

Select the fabric

3/8 yard each of 12 assorted light prints or plaids

3/8 yard each of 12 assorted dark prints or plaids

1-1/2 yards gold/orange for borders and binding

4-1/3 yards for backing

Cut the fabric

1. From light prints or plaids, cut 1—11" strip; from the strip, cut 78—6×11" rectangles.

2. From dark prints or plaids, cut 1—11" strip; from the strip, cut 78—6×11" rectangles.

3. From gold/orange, cut 11—2-1/2" strips; sew 7 strips together end to end. From the length, cut 2—60-1/2" and 2—56-1/2" lengths. Set aside remaining 4 strips.

   8—2-1/2" strips; sew the strips end to end for a continuous binding length.

Sew 312 half-square triangles

1. Right sides facing, place light 6×11" rectangles on dark 6×11" rectangles. On wrong side of the light fabric, draw 2—5" square grids with a sharp fabric pencil or fine-point fabric pen. Draw a diagonal line from corner to corner on each 5" square (refer to *page 19*). From each rectangle, you will make 4 half-square triangles.

2. Sew 1/4" from each side of the diagonal lines. Cut on all of the diagonal and grid lines using a rotary cutter and ruler or scissors.

3. Press seams flat. Open the light triangles. pressing seams toward the dark triangle.

4. Trim each triangle square unit to 4-1/2" square, maintaining seams in the corners of each unit.

Assemble the quilt top in rows and sections

1. Noting triangle square light and dark positions, lay out 10 rows of 8 units each for the center of the quilt top. Join the units in each row. Press seams of each row in the opposite direction from the preceding row. Sew the row together. Press seams in one direction.

2. Sew the first 2-1/2×40-1/2" gold/orange inner border to each long side; press seams toward the borders. Sew 2-1/2×36-1/2" inner borders to the top and bottom; press seams toward the borders.

3. For the double row of triangle squares beyond the first inner border, lay out units in 2 double rows each of 13 units and 2 double rows each of 11 units, noting light/dark positions.

4. Sew 11-unit double rows to each side. Press seams toward the inner border. Sew 13-unit double rows to the top and bottom. Press seams toward the inner border.

5. For the second inner border, sew a 2-1/2×60-1/2" length to each long side; press. Sew a 2-1/2×56-1/2" length to the top and to the bottom; press.

6. For the outer double rows of triangle squares, lay out and join 2 double rows each of 16 units and 2 double rows each of 18 units, noting light/dark positions.

7. Sew shorter rows to each side of the quilt top, along the last inner border. Press seams toward the border. Sew a longer row to the top and to the bottom, press seams toward border.

8. Press the quilt top. Stitch close to the edge around the quilt to stabilize for layering and binding.

Finish the quilt

Refer to General Instructions, *pages 9–15,* to layer, baste, quilt, and bind the quilt.

Row and Border Assembly

Horizon Sails Finished Quilt Assembly

Trellis

This stitched version of a garden structure may inspire you to search through garden catalogs—even when the snow is swirling and blowing outdoors.

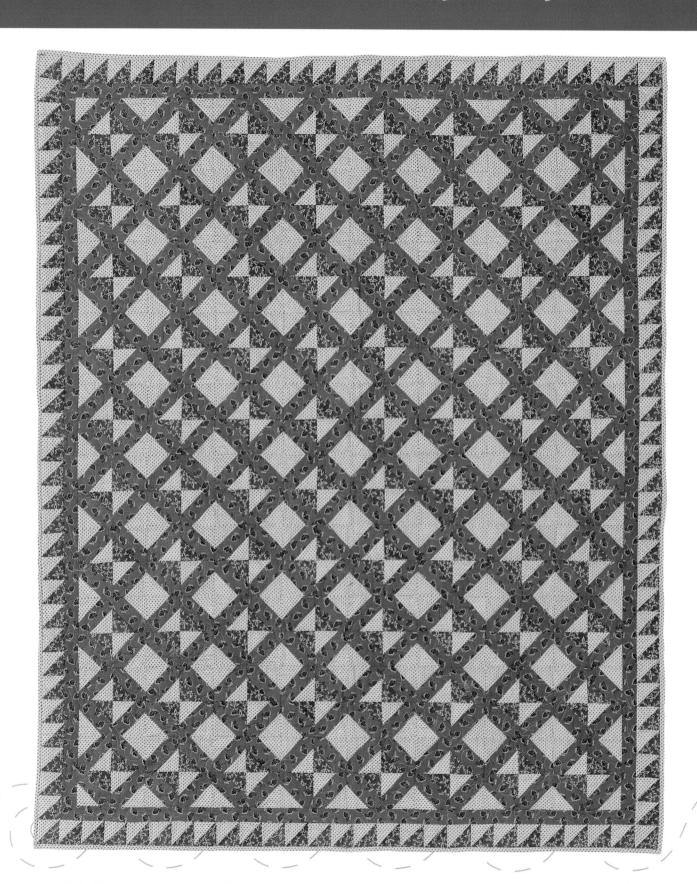

Finished size 54×66"

Select the fabric

3-1/2 yards pink print

1-1/2 yards green print

*4 yards off-white print
for background and binding*

3-3/4 yards for backing

Cut the fabric

1. From pink print, cut
   30—3-1/2" strips; from the strips cut
   320—3-1/2" squares for blocks.

   6—1-3/4" strips; sew the strips end to
   end for a continuous length.

2. From green print, cut
   5—2-1/2"strips; from the strips cut
   80—2-1/2" squares for blocks.

   5—15×11-1/2" rectangles

3. From off-white print, cut
   30—2-1/2" strips; from the strips cut
   480—2-1/2" squares for blocks.

   5—15×11-1/2" rectangles

   6—2-1/2" strips; sew the strips end
   to end for continuous binding length.

Sew Trellis blocks and triangle squares

1. Draw a diagonal line from corner to
   corner on the wrong side of a 2-1/2"
   white square. Using template-free-
   angle piecing, align a 2-1/2" off-white
   square on the corner of a 3-1/2" pink
   square, right sides together. Sew on
   the drawn line. Press, trim the seam to

1/4" on the white fabric *only*. Press the
off-white triangle open. Sew a 2-1/2"
off-white square to the opposite
corner. Press, trim, press the triangle
open. Repeat to make 160 white-pink-
white Unit A blocks.

2. Make 160 white-pink-green Unit B
   blocks, following the directions for
   Unit A in Step 1, *above.*

3. Right sides together, align pairs of
   off-white 15×11-1/2" rectangles with
   green 15×11-1/2" rectangles. On the
   wrong side of each off-white
   rectangle, draw a grid of 12—3-1/2"
   squares (4×3). Draw diagonally in one
   direction through the squares.

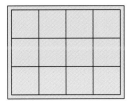 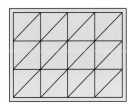

4. Sew 1/4" on both sides of each
   diagonal line. Cut on all of the drawn
   lines to make 120 Unit C triangle
   square blocks. Trim each off-
   white/green triangle square to 2-1/2".

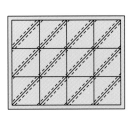 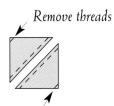

Remove threads

Remove threads

Assemble Trellis blocks

1. Sew each Unit A to each Unit B, noting color placement. Press seams toward Unit B.

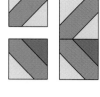

2. Sew together two joined units, reversing the direction of one joined unit so that the green triangles meet at the center. Make 80 blocks. Press seams flat or open.

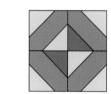

Assemble the quilt top

1. Noting color placement, lay out and sew 10 rows of 8 blocks each, carefully butting block seams. Press the seams of each row in the opposite direction from the preceding row.

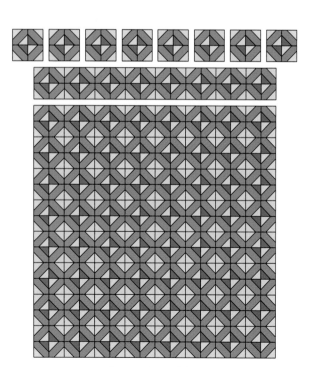

Row Assembly

2. Sew the rows together, matching and butting seams for a flat finish. Press the finished seams to lay flat, pressing in the direction of least resistance.

3. Cut 2 pink 60-1/2" inner border strips; sew one to each side. Press. Cut 2 pink 51" inner border strips. Sew one to the top and bottom. Press seams toward the borders.

4. For the sawtooth border, join off-white/green Unit C blocks in 2 rows of 31 units and 2 rows of 27 units, noting color placement. Press seams toward green triangles.

5. Sew a sawtooth border to each side, then to the top and bottom. Press seams toward the pink border.

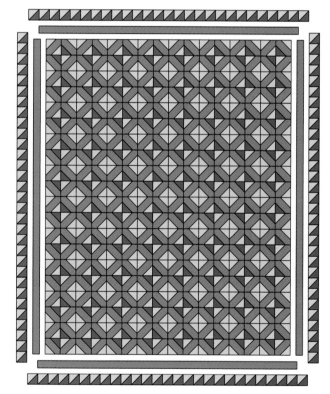

Border Assembly

Finish the quilt

Refer to General Instructions, *pages 9–15*, to layer, baste, quilt, and bind the quilt.

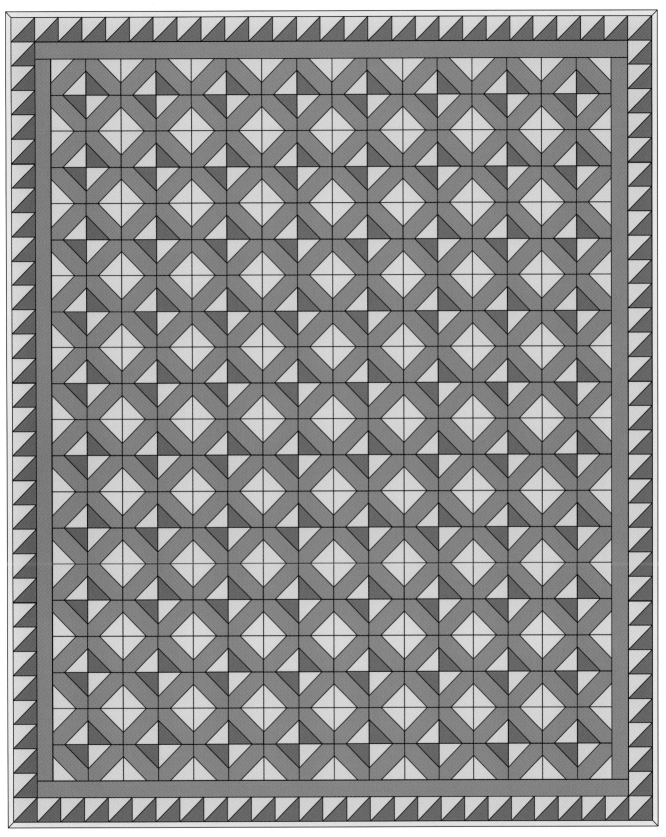

Trellis Finished Quilt Assembly

Square in a Square

Like a diamond tucked in a box, colorful rectangles frame this Log Cabin version.
Use an armload of assorted fabric to create this sun and shadow delight.

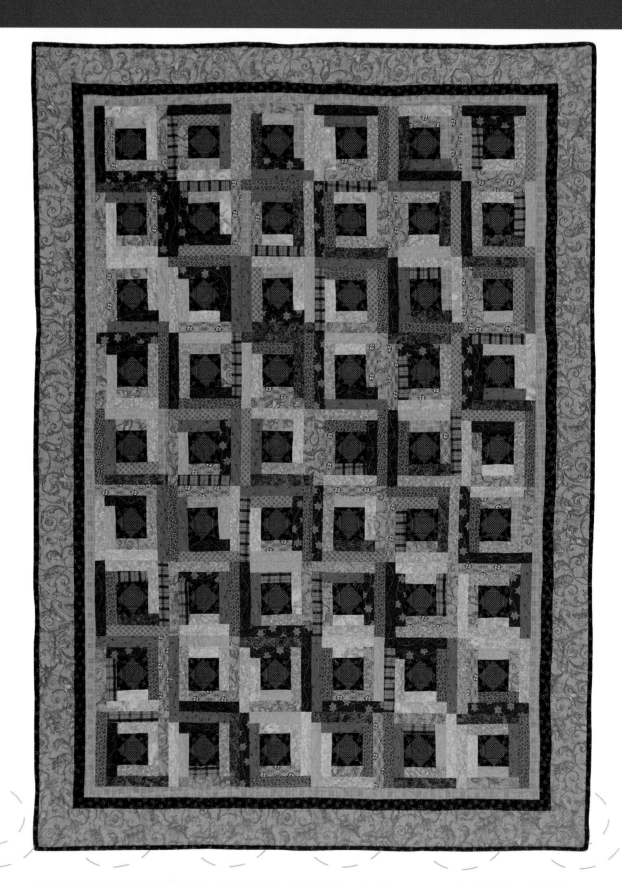

Finished size 53×73"
54—7" square blocks

Select the fabric

1/4 yard green check for center squares

1/2 yard medium brown for center triangles

*1-1/2 yards black print for center triangles,
inner border, and binding*

*1/2 yard each of 4 assorted light prints
for Log Cabin rectangles*

*1/2 yard each of 4 assorted medium prints
for Log Cabin rectangles*

1/3 yard light print for first inner border

1 yard green print for wide outer border

3-1/2 yards backing

Cut the fabric

1. From green check cut
   3—2" strips; from the strips cut
   54—2" squares.

2. From medium brown cut
   6—2" strips; from the strips cut
   108—2" squares. Diagonally cut each
   square for 216 half-square triangles.

3. From black print cut
   14—2-1/2" strips; from 7 of the strips
   cut 108—2-1/2" squares. Diagonally
   cut each square for 216 half-square
   triangles. Sew the remaining 7—2-1/2"
   strips end to end for continuous
   binding length.

   6—1-1/2" strips; sew the strips
   together end to end for a continuous
   length.

4. From assorted light fabrics cut
   7—1-1/2" strips; from the strips cut
   and separate by lengths:
   54—3-1/2" rectangles
   54—4-1/2" rectangles
   54—5-1/2" rectangles
   54—6-1/2" rectangles

5. From assorted medium fabrics cut
   9—1-1/2" strips; from the strips cut
   and separate by lengths:
   54—4-1/2" rectangles
   54—5-1/2" rectangles
   54—6-1/2" rectangles
   54—7-1/2" rectangles

6. From light for inner border, cut
   6—1-1/2" strips; sew the strips
   together end to end for a continuous
   length.

7. From green print for outer border, cut
   7—4" strips; sew the strips together
   end to end for a continuous length.

Sew 54 Square in a Square Log Cabin Blocks

*Tip: For perfect points, sew triangles to squares from
the backside, with visible seam intersections. Sew
across the intersection, one thread to the outside.*

1. Right sides together, align raw edges,
   triangle points extending evenly
   beyond each side. Sew a brown
   triangle to opposite sides of each
   green 2" square. Press seams toward
   the triangle. Use the chain-piecing
   method (see General Instructions,
   page 13) to sew triangles to squares.
   Press triangles open.

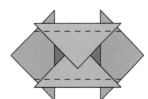

2. Sew brown triangles to opposite sides of the units; press triangles open. Trim the unit to 2-5/8" square.

3. Right sides together, align raw edges and allow triangle points to extend evenly beyond each side of the square. Sew a black triangle to opposite sides of each of the 54—2-5/8" center units. Press seams toward the black triangles.

4. Sew black triangles to opposite sides of the units; press triangles open. Trim the units to 3-1/2" square.

5. Sewing clockwise around the 3-1/2" center squares, join Log Cabin rectangles in the following order, pressing seams toward the most recently rectangle added:
   3-1/2" light
   4-1/2" light
   4-1/2" dark
   5-1/2" dark
   5-1/2" light
   6-1/2" light
   6-1/2" dark
   7-1/2" dark

Blocks should measure 7-1/2" square; trim blocks to uniform size.

Assemble rows and borders

1. Lay out the blocks to create zigzag patterns of light and dark in 9 rows of 6 blocks each.

2. Join the blocks in each row. Press seams open or in one direction, alternating seam direction with adjacent rows.

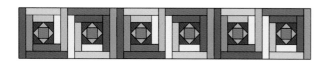

3. Join the rows, matching and abutting seams. Press the quilt top.

4. Measure the quilt lengthwise through the center. Cut and sew light inner borders to each side of the quilt; press seams toward the border. Measure widthwise through the center. Cut and sew borders to the top and bottom; press seams toward borders.

5. Follow Step 4 to sew black print borders to the sides, then top and bottom. Press toward the black border.

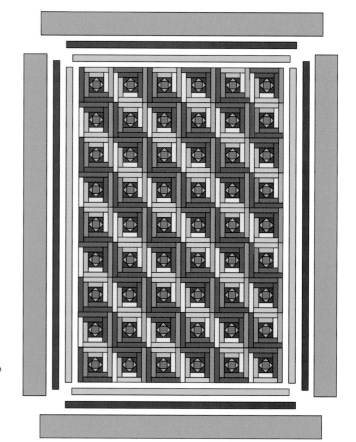

Row and Border Assembly

6. Follow Step 4 to sew green 4" borders to the sides, then top and bottom. Press seams toward the outer border.

Finish the quilt

Refer to General Instructions, *pages 9–15*, to layer, baste, quilt, and bind the quilt.

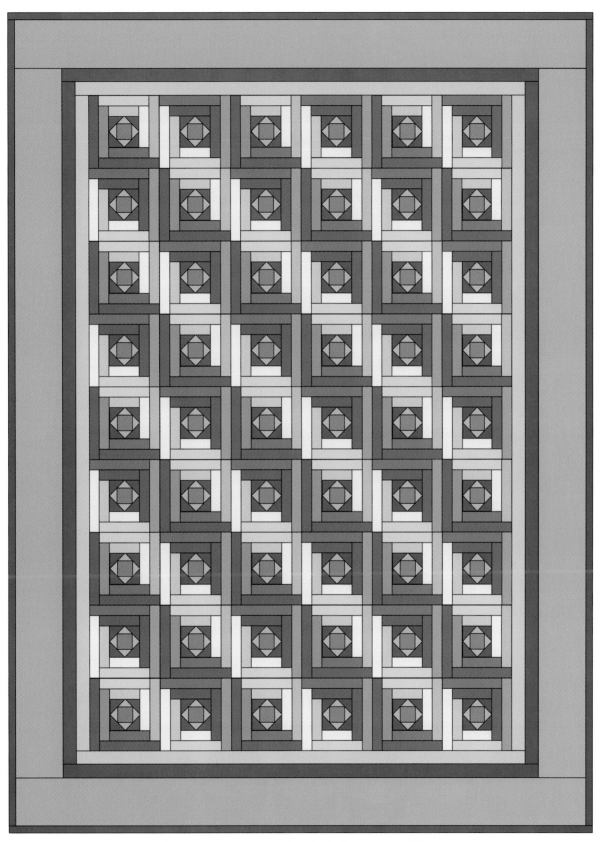

Square in a Square Finished Quilt Assembly

Star Flower

These bright harbingers of spring arise from the background, like welcome blooms peeping through snow cover. You'll love the quick technique to make this quilt.

Finished size 52×64"

Select fabric and materials

1/3 yard each of 11 assorted bright fabrics

2-1/4 yards white print

1/3 yard green for inner border

1/2 yard black for binding

3-1/2 yards backing

4 yards lightweight fusible adhesive

Template plastic

Make the templates

1. Trace Templates A and B, *page 87*, onto template plastic. Cut out on the lines.

2. Trace 110 of template A and 64 of Template B to fusible adhesive film.

Cut the fabric

1. From each assorted bright fabric, cut 6—6-1/2" squares for star flowers.

2. From white print, cut 6—4-1/2" outer border strips; sew the strips end to end for a continuous length. From the length, cut 2—52-1/2" and 2—56-1/2" lengths.

   4—1-1/2" inner border corner squares.

3. From dark, cut 5—1-1/2" strips; sew the strips end to end for a continuous length. From the length, cut 2—44-1/2" and 2—54-1/2" lengths.

4. From black, cut 6—2-1/2" strips; sew the strips end to end for a continuous binding length.

Assemble Star blocks

1. Lay out 63—6-1/2" squares in 9 rows of 7 squares each.

2. Sew together each row of squares, press seams of each row in alternate direction from adjacent rows.

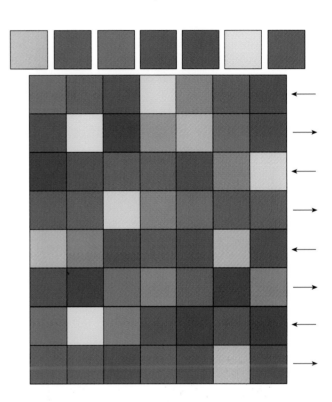

3. Sew the rows together, butting seams. Press seams in one direction.

4. Following fusing material manufacturer's directions, fuse 110 of Template A and 32 (*half of the traced and fused half-diamonds*) of Template B to white print fabric. Cut out the fused fabric on the lines.

5. Place and fuse Template A vertically over block seam lines, points meeting at row seams (trim points if necessary).

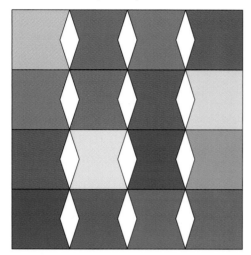

6. Place and fuse Template A horizontally along seam lines; trim points for intersecting points.

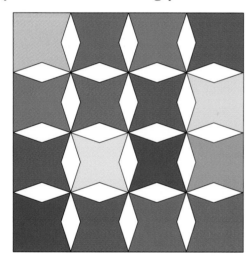

7. Place and fuse Template B along the outer rows, trim intersecting points.

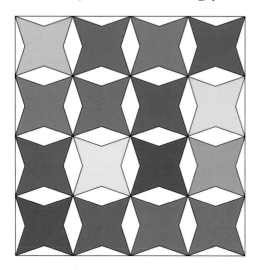

8. Using matching thread, hand or machine appliqué around the fused diamonds and half-diamonds.

Sew on the borders

1. Right sides together and matching raw edges, place a white print 1-1/2" square on each end of a green 44-1/2" inner border strip. Mark and sew diagonally across the white print squares. Cut away 1/4" from the sewn lines on the dark strip *only*. Press to set the seams. Open the white print squares; press the seams flat.

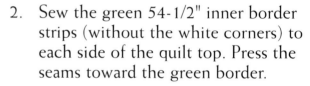

2. Sew the green 54-1/2" inner border strips (without the white corners) to each side of the quilt top. Press the seams toward the green border.

3. Noting position of the white print triangle, sew the green 44-1/2" inner borders to the top and bottom of the quilt top. Press seams toward the green border.

4. Lay the 4-1/2×56-1/2" side and 4-1/2×56-1/2" top and bottom outer borders evenly along the quilt top (see Row and Border Assembly, *opposite*).

5. Fuse the remaining 32 half-diamonds to assorted bright fabrics. Cut out on the lines.

6. Position the bright half-diamonds along inner side of the white border, aligning with adjacent white half-diamonds beyond the inner border. Trim points as necessary.

7. Appliqué around the bright half-diamonds with coordinating or contrasting threads.

8. Sew the borders to each side, taking care to align half-diamonds by pinning at critical points. Press seams toward the inner borders. Sew the top and bottom borders to the quilt top, aligning half-diamonds. Press seams toward the inner borders.

Finish the quilt

Refer to General Instructions, *pages 9–15*, to layer, baste, quilt, and bind the quilt.

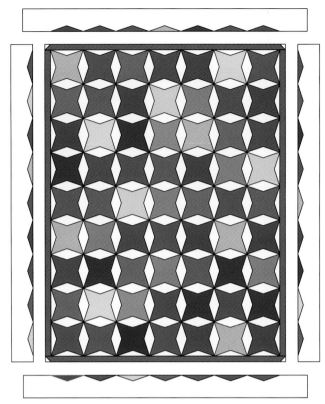

Row and Border Assembly

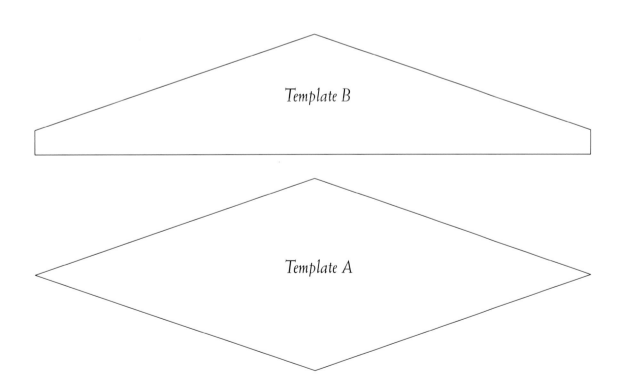

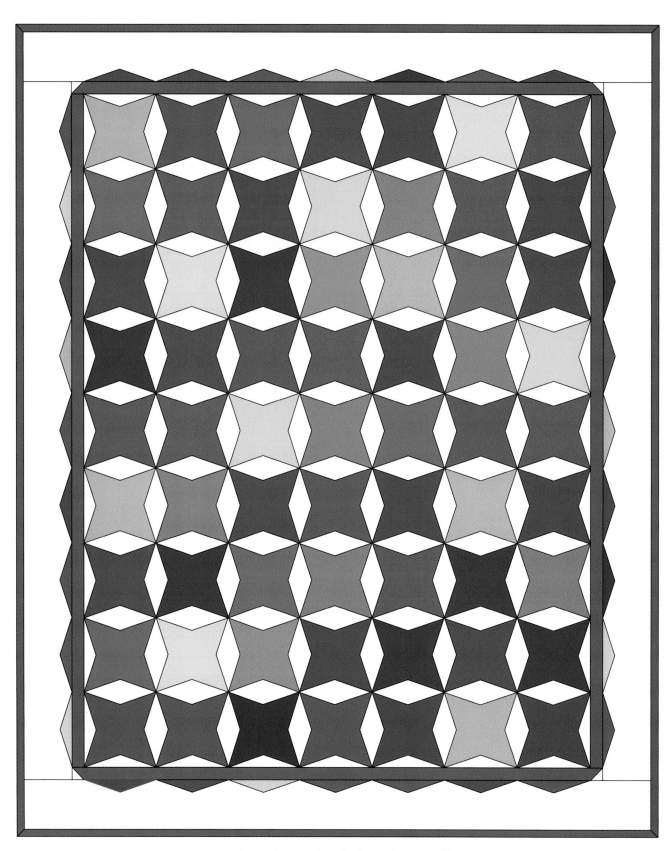

Star Flower Finished Quilt Assembly

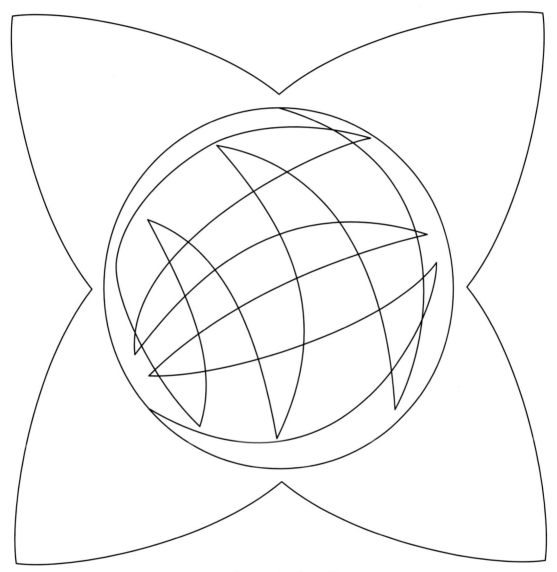

Star Flower Quilting Design

Sunshine Flower

Ever-popular sunflowers burst forth on this dimensional tri-color quilt. Framed in earthy brown and a bright checkerboard, this quilt will brighten any decor.

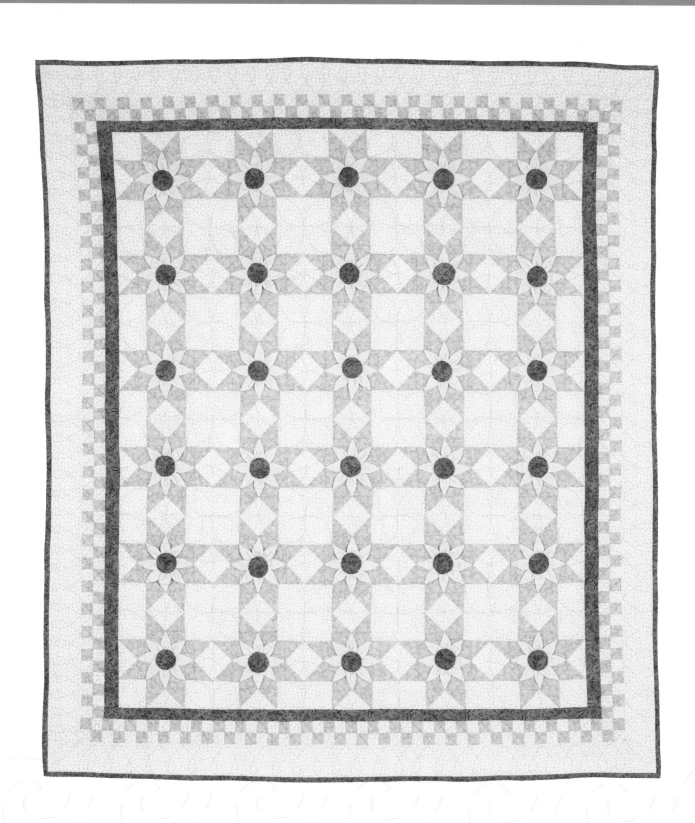

Finished size 55×63"
30—8" finished blocks

Select fabric and materials

2-1/2 yards yellow for flowers and checkerboard border

3 yards white with yellow print for background, checkerboard, and outer border

2-3/4 yards solid white for flower petals

1-1/2 yards light brown for flower centers, inner border, and binding

3-1/2 yards for backing

Template plastic

Prepare the templates

1. Trace Template A and Template B onto template plastic. Cut out on traced lines.

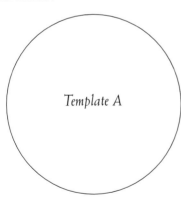

Template A

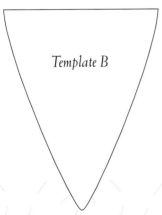

Template B

Cut the fabric

1. From yellow, cut
   19—2-1/4" strips; from the strips cut 240—2-1/4" squares.

   7—4" strips. From 2 of the 4" strips cut 60—1-1/4" rectangles; from 5 of the 4" strips cut 30—5-1/2" rectangles.

   8—1-1/2" strips for the checkerboard.

2. From white with yellow print, cut
   7—4-1/2" strips; from the strips cut 120—2-1/4" rectangles.

   9—3" strips; from the strips cut 120—3" squares.

   6—3-1/2" strips; sew the strips end to end for a continuous length.

   8—1-1/2 strips for the checkerboard.

3. From solid white, cut
   11—8-1/2" strips; from the strips, cut 32—13" rectangles for flower petals.

4. From light brown, cut
   2—5-1/2" strips, from the strips cut 6—12-1/2" flower center rectangles.

   3—1-3/4" strips; sew the strips for a continuous length. Cut inner border 2—51-1/2" lengths for the sides.

   3—1-1/2" strips; sew the strips for a continuous length. Cut inner border 2—45-1/2" lengths, top and bottom.

   6—2-1/2" strips; sew the strips end to end for a continuous binding.

Sew 30 Sunshine Flower blocks

Note: Make 120 Flying Geese units; use 4 to make each Sunshine Flower block.

1. Right sides together, match raw edges and place a 2-1/4" yellow square along

one side of a 2-1/4×4" white with yellow print rectangle. Draw a diagonal line from top to bottom. Sew on the line; trim the seam on the yellow square *only*; press the seam toward the yellow triangle.

2. Place a 2-1/4" yellow square on the opposite side of the rectangle, draw a diagonal line, sew and trim. Press the triangle open to complete a Flying Geese unit. Make 120 units.

3. Noting placement, sew a 1-1/4×4" yellow rectangle to each of 60 Flying Geese units. Press seams toward the yellow rectangle.

4. Sew a 3" white with yellow print rectangle to each narrow side of the 60 Flying Geese units assembled in Step 3.

5. Noting placement, sew a Flying Geese unit to each narrow side of a 4×5-1/2" yellow rectangle. Press seams toward the yellow rectangle.

6. Lay out 2 units from Step 4 with one Unit from Step 5. Match seams and raw edges and sew the units to complete a 30 Sunshine Blocks. Each block should measure 8-1/2" square.

Cut and sew 30 flower centers and 240 petals

1. Right sides together, stack 3 pairs of 5-1/2×12-1/2" light brown rectangles; press the fabric. Trace 10 Template A circles, spaced 1/2" apart, on one side of the doubled fabric. Set the machine stitching to a short length. Stitch on the lines. Cut around the circles, leaving a 1/8" seam allowance all around. Make a 1" slit in one side of the circle, turn the fabric to the right side, and press. Make 30 light brown Flower Centers.

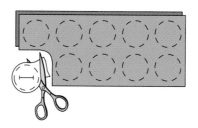

2. Right sides together, stack 16 pairs of 8-1/2×13" white rectangles; press the fabric. Trace 15 Template B petals on one side of each doubled fabric, spacing petals approximately 1" apart. Stitch along the curved lines of the shape, leaving the bottom open for turning. Cut out the shapes, leaving about 1/8" seam allowance all around. Turn petals to right side; finger press.

3. Make an inverted pleat in the base of each petal, making the base approximately 3/4" across. Baste close to the raw edge.

4. Space and pin petals around the center of the block. Place a flower center to cover the base of the petals; mark the position. Remove the flower center.

Baste the base of the petals and tack the point, for a dimensional appearance. Reposition the center and appliqué it to cover the base of the petals.

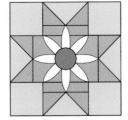

Assemble the rows

1. Lay out the blocks in 6 rows of 5 blocks each.

2. Sew together each row of blocks, butting Flying Geese points for smooth seams. Press the seams of each row in alternate directions than adjacent rows.

3. Sew the rows together, butting block seams of blocks and Flying Geese points for smooth seams. Press the seams in one direction.

Sew on the Inner Border

1. Sew a 51-1/2" light brown strip to each long side of the quilt top. Press seams toward the border.

2. Sew each 45-1/2" light brown strip to the top and bottom of the quilt top. Press seams toward the border.

Sew on the Checkerboard

1. For the checkerboard border, sew together a 1-1/2" yellow strip and a 1-1/2" white with yellow strip to make 8 strips sets. Press seams toward the yellow strips. From the strip sets, cut 204—1-1/2" segments.

2. Sew together 2 rows of 53 segments for the sides and 2 rows 49 segments for the top and bottom. Adjust the lengths to fit.

3. Sew the checkerboard sides, then the top and bottom, to the quilt top. Press seams toward the inner border.

4. Measure the quilt top lengthwise through the center. Cut and sew 3-1/2" white with yellow print outer border strips to each side. Press seams toward the wide border. Measure the quilt top widthwise through the center. Cut and sew outer border strips to the top and bottom. Press seams toward the outer border.

Row and Border Assembly

Finish the quilt

Refer to General Instructions, *pages 9–15*, to layer, baste, quilt, and bind the quilt.

Sunshine Flower Finished Quilt Assembly

Sunshine Flower Quilting Design

Watermelon Pie

Yummy, juicy watermelon slices—without all the seeds to mess with.
This colorful rendition could serve as a Christmas quilt or colorful table cover.

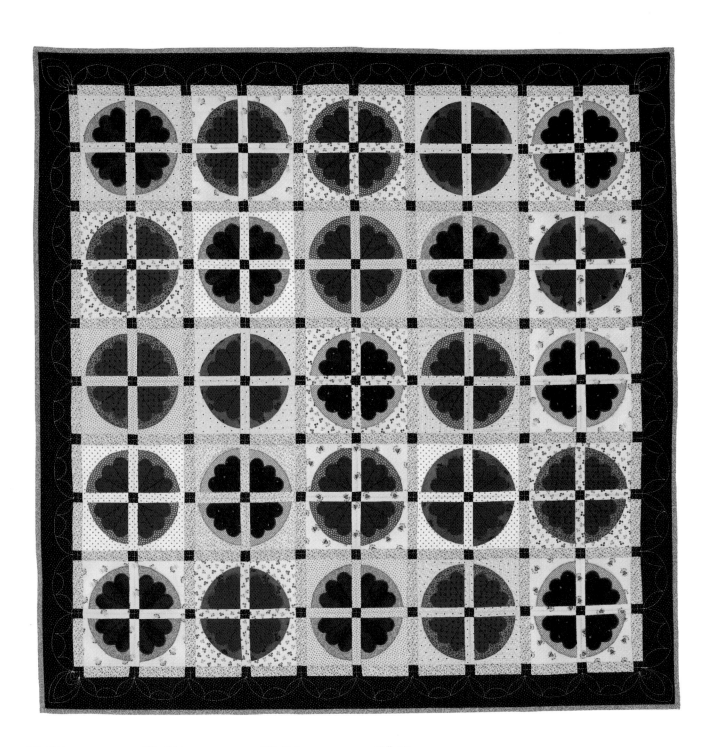

Finished size 48-1/4" square

Select the fabric

3/8 yard each of 5 assorted lights
for background

5/8 yard light green print for sashing

2/3 yard dark green for corner squares
and outer border

1/4 yard each of 5 assorted greens

1/4 yard each of 5 assorted reds

1/2 yard green for binding

3 yards of backing

7-1/2 yards of lightweight fusible webbing

Black embroidery floss

Cut the fabric

1. From each assorted light for
   background, cut
   3—4" strips; from 2 strips cut
   20—4" squares; from 1 strip cut
   20—1-1/4" rectangles (for a total of
   100—4" squares for melon block and
   100—1-1/4" sashing strip rectangles).

2. From small green print for sashing, cut
   12—1-1/4" strips; from the strips cut
   120—4" rectangles.

3. From dark green, cut
   4—1-1/4" strips; from the strips cut
   121—1-1/4" squares.

   5—3" strips for the outer border. Sew
   the strips end to end for a continuous
   length. From the length, cut
   2—43-3/4" side lengths and
   2—48-3/4" top and bottom lengths.

Make 25 Watermelon Blocks

1. Trace Watermelon Template A,
   page 103, onto fusible webbing,
   allowing at least 1/2" between each
   shape, to make 100 quarter circles.
   Note: *If hand-appliquéing, add 1/4" all
   around the templates.* Cut out the quarter
   circles 1/4" outside the line.

2. Following fusing manufacturer's
   directions, fuse 20 quarter circles to
   the wrong side of each of the assorted
   green fabrics. Cut out the quarter
   circles on the drawn line. Fuse each
   quarter circle to a 4" square.

3. Trace Watermelon Template B,
   page 103, onto fusible adhesive,
   allowing at least 1/2" between each
   shape, to make 100 melon shapes.
   Cut out the shapes approximately
   1/4" outside the line. Fuse 20 melon
   shapes to assorted red fabrics.

4. Cut out the melon shapes on the
   drawn lines. Layer and fuse the red
   melon shapes to the green quarter
   circle rinds on the 4" squares.

5. Appliqué by hand or machine around
   the outer edges of
   the rind and melon.
   Use black
   embroidery floss
   to sew pie slice lines
   through the melon.

6. Match melon
   background fabrics
   to the
   1-1/4" sashing strip rectangles.

7. Join 2 quarter
   block segments
   with 1-1/4"
   sashing strip
   rectangles. Press
   seams toward
   the sashing
   strips.

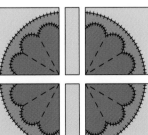

8. Sew a 1-1/4" sashing strip rectangle to each side of a 1-1/4" dark green square. Sew the joined piece to the inner long edge of each half block to make one Watermelon Pie block.

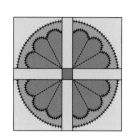

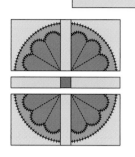

Sash and border the Watermelon Pie Blocks

1. Sew together 6 sashing strips using 11—1-1/4" dark green squares and 10—4×1-1/4" light green rectangles.

2. Sew together 30 sashing units using 1—1-1/4" dark green square and 2—4×1-1/4" light green rectangles.

3. Lay out 5 rows of 5 Watermelon Blocks, short sashing strips between the blocks.

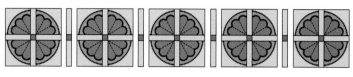

4. Join the blocks with the short sashing strips to complete each horizontal row. Press the seams flat.

5. Join the rows of blocks with the long sashing strips. Press the seams flat.

6. Sew the 2—3×43-3/4" outer border strips to each side of the quilt top. Press seams toward the border. Sew the 2—3×48-3/4" outer border strips to the top and bottom of the quilt top. Press seams toward the border.

Finish the quilt

Refer to General Instructions, *pages 9–15*, to layer, baste, quilt, and bind the quilt.

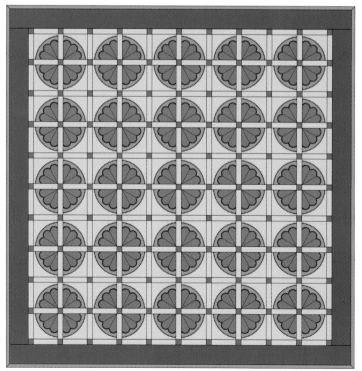

Watermelon Pie Finished Quilt Assembly

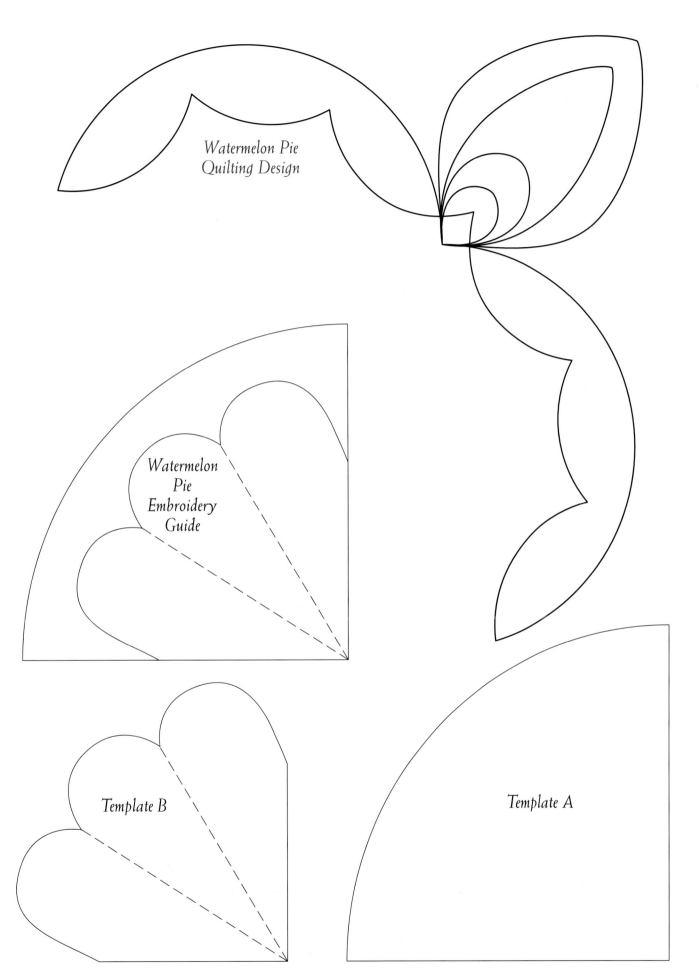

Watermelon Pie
Quilting Design

Watermelon
Pie
Embroidery
Guide

Template B

Template A

Window Boxes

This homespun beauty pays tribute to wonderful shirting plaids and flannels, gathered in a collage of color and texture. Grab the scrap bag and have fun piecing.

Finished size 60×72-1/2"
20—11" finished blocks

Select the fabric

*1/4 yard each of 35 or more assorted
homespun or flannel plaids*

5/8 yard dark plaid for binding

3-3/8 yards for backing

Cut the fabric

1. From assorted fabrics, cut
   86—3" center squares for blocks and
   borders.

   2"-wide strips in varying lengths to
   piece for Scrappy Border B.

   1-1/2"-wide strips in varying lengths to
   piece for the 53" Scrappy Borders A,
   C, D, and E.

   20 of each of the following lengths to
   frame the center squares for blocks
   (cut 1 compete set from the same
   fabric to frame each block).

   Set 1:
   Strips 1 and 2—1×3"
   Strips 3 and 4—1×4"

   Set 2:
   Strips 5 and 6—1-1/2×4"
   Strips 7 and 8—1-1/2×6"

   Set 3:
   Strips 9 and 10—1×6"
   Strips 11 and 12—1×7"

   Set 4:
   Strips 13 and 14—1-1/2×7"
   Strips 15 and 16—1-1/2×9"

   Set 5:
   Strips 17 and 18—1-1/2× 9"
   Strips 19 and 20—1-1/2×11"

   To frame the squares for the border
   blocks, cut 66 of Set 1 (same fabric
   for each block, duplicating fabrics
   as necessary).

2. From dark plaid for binding, cut
   7—2-1/2" strips; sew the strips end to
   end for a continuous binding length.

Sew 20 Window Box blocks

1. Sew strips to the center block
   consecutively. Press after adding each
   set of lengths.

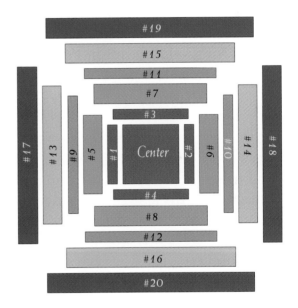

2. Square each block to measure 11-1/2".

3. Lay out the blocks in 5 rows of
   4 blocks each. Join the blocks in each
   row. Press seams of each row in the
   opposite direction from adjacent rows.

4. Sew the block rows together, butting seams for a smooth finish. Press seams.

Piece Scrappy Borders A, B, and C

1. For Border A, sew 1-1/2"-wide strips end to end. Cut 2—44-1/2" top and bottom lengths and 2—53" side lengths. Sew the borders to the quilt top, sides first, then top and bottom. Press.

2. For Border B, sew 2"-wide strips end to end. Cut 2—47-1/2" top and bottom lengths and 2—55" side lengths. Sew the borders, sides first, then top and bottom next to Border A. Press the seams.

3. For Border C, sew 1-1/2"-wide strips end to end. Cut 2—49-1/2" top and bottom lengths and 2—58" sides lengths (adjust to fit). Sew sides, then

top and bottom to quilt, next to Border B. Press the seams.

Piece 66 Border blocks

1. Sew Set 1 strips to each of the 66—3" center blocks for the border, pressing after each set of lengths.

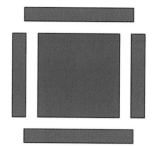

2. Assemble the row, rotating blocks 90 degrees from adjacent blocks. Sew 2—16 block strips for the top and bottom and 2—17 block strips for the sides of the quilt top. Press the seams in one direction.

3. Adjusting length to fit, sew Border Block strips to the sides, then the top and bottom. Press seams toward Border C.

Piece Scrappy Borders D and E

1. For Border D, sew 1-1/2"-wide strips end to end. From the length, cut 2—58-1/2" top and bottom lengths and 2—67" side lengths. Sew the sides, then the top and bottom. Press seams toward the Block Border.

2. For Border E, sew 1-1/2"-wide strips end to end. From the length, cut 2—60-1/2" top and bottom lengths and 2—69" side lengths. Sew the

sides, then the top and bottom borders to the quilt. Press the seams toward Border D.

3. Sew a basting stitch all around the quilt top 1/8" from the edge.

Finish the quilt

Refer to General Instructions, *pages 9–15*, to layer, baste, quilt, and bind the quilt.

Window Boxes Finished Quilt Assembly

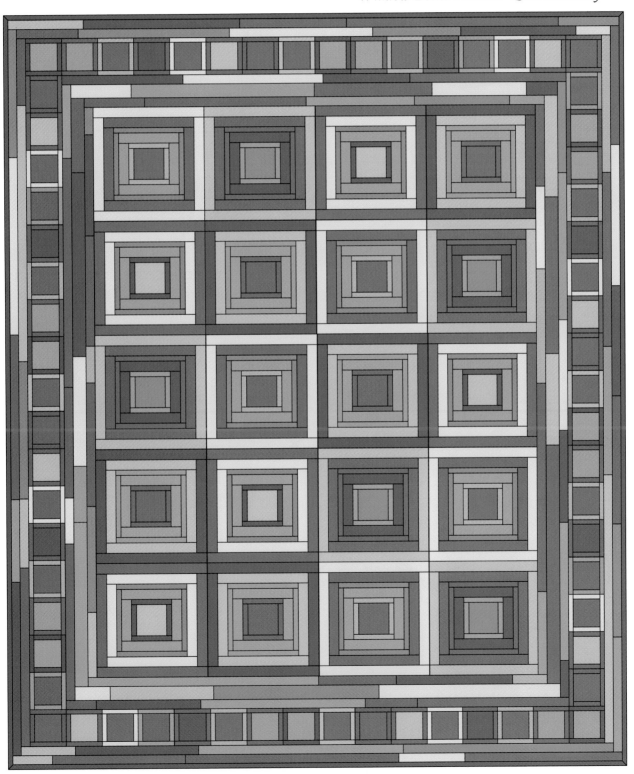

Window Boxes
Quilting Design

Window Boxes
Quilting Design

Autumn Lights

During late summer and early autumn, nature provides brilliant displays of contrasting color. Duplicate those intense hues in this easy-to-piece quilt.

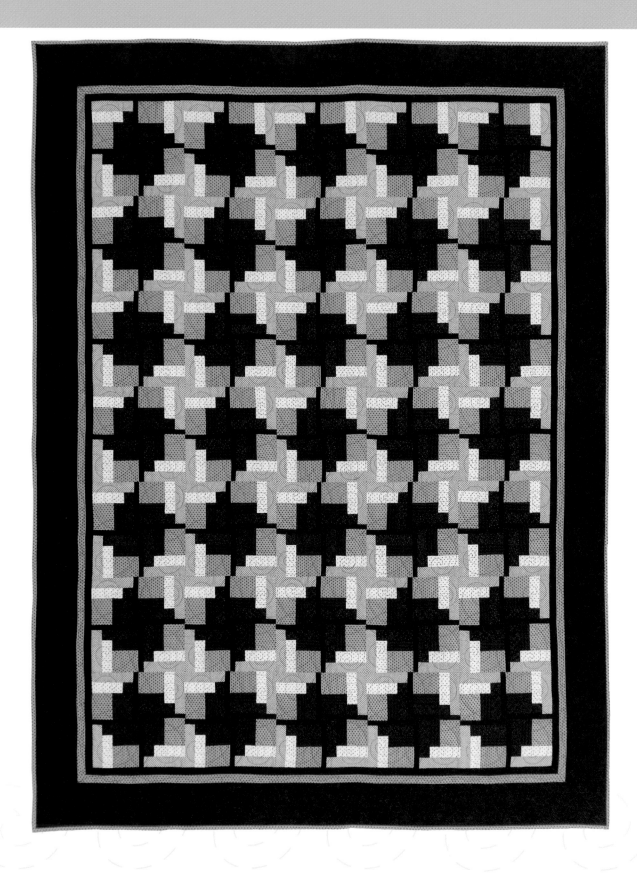

Finished size 57-1/2×75-1/2"
35—9" square finished blocks

Select the fabric

2 yards gold print

1/2 yard red print No. 1

3/4 yard red print No. 2

5/8 yard light beige print

3/4 yard beige print

7/8 yard dark red print No. 1

1-1/4 yards dark red print No. 2

3-1/2 yards of backing

Cut the fabric

1. From gold print, cut
   17—2-1/2" strips; from 10 strips, cut
   140—3" rectangles; sew 7 strips end to
   end for a continuous binding length.

   6—2" strips; sew the strips end to
   end for a continuous length for
   inner borders.

2. From red print No. 1, cut
   10—1-1/2" strips; from the strips cut
   140—3" rectangles.

3. From red print No. 2, cut
   14—1-1/2" strips; from the strips cut
   140—4" rectangles.

4. From light beige print, cut
   12—1-1/2" strips; from the strips cut
   140—3-1/2" rectangles.

5. From beige print, cut
   16—1-1/2" strips; from the strips cut
   140—4-1/2" rectangles.

6. From dark red print No. 1, cut
   18—1" strips; from the strips cut
   140—5" rectangles.

7. From dark red print No. 2, cut
   6—1-1/4" strips; sew the strips end
   to end for a continuous length for
   inner borders.

   7—4-1/2" strips; sew the strip end
   to end for a continuous length for
   outer borders.

Sew 140 quarter units to make 35 Autumn Light blocks

1. Sew each red print 1-1/2×3" rectangle
   to one long edge of a gold print
   2-1/2×3" rectangle. Press seams toward
   the red fabric.

2. Sew each light beige 1-1/2×3-1/2"
   rectangle to the gold and red unit,
   noting placement. Press seams toward
   the light beige fabric.

3. Sew each red print 1-1/2×4" rectangle
   to the bottom edge of the piece
   unit. Press seams toward the second
   red fabric.

4. Sew each beige 1-1/2×4-1/2" rectangle to the right edge of the pieced unit. Press seams toward the beige fabric.

5. Sew each dark red print 1×5" rectangle to the bottom edge of pieced unit. Press seams toward the dark red fabric.

6. Lay out 4 quarter units for each block, placing narrow dark red strips in the center of each block.

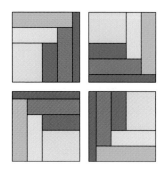

7. Sew the blocks together, halves first, then join the halves to make 35 blocks. Press seams to lie flat.

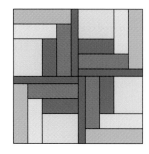

Assemble rows and borders

1. Lay out 7 rows of 5 blocks each. Sew together each row of blocks. Press seams of adjacent rows in opposite directions. Join the rows. Press seams in one direction.

2. Machine stitch around the quilt top, 1/8" from the edge.

3. From the dark red 1-1/4" continuous strip, cut 2—47" lengths and 2—63-1/2" lengths. Sew 63-1/2" lengths to each side; press seams toward border. Sew 47" lengths to the top and bottom; press.

4. From the 2" gold print strip, cut 2—52-1/2" lengths and 2—65-1/2" lengths. Sew 65-1/2" lengths to each side; press seams toward the gold border. Sew 52-1/2" lengths to the top and bottom; press seams toward the gold border.

5. From 4-1/2" dark red print strip, cut 2—68" side lengths and 2—58" top and bottom lengths. Sew 68" lengths to each side; press seams toward outer border. Sew 58" lengths to the top and bottom; press toward outer border.

Finish the quilt

Refer to General Instructions, *pages 9–15*, to layer, baste, quilt, and bind the quilt.

Row and Border Assembly

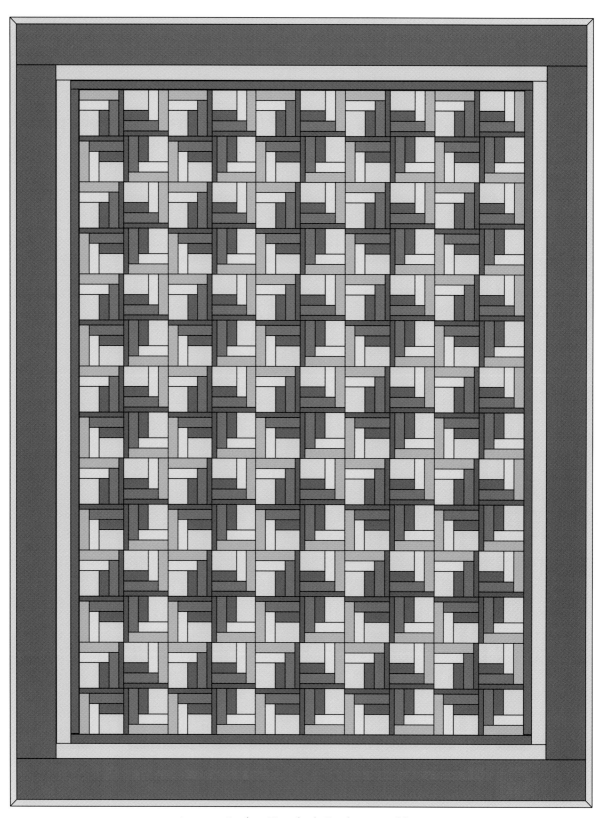

Autumn Lights Finished Quilt Assembly

Autumn Lights Quilting Design

Homestead Hospitality

*The universal symbol of welcome is depicted in rows of spiraling triangles—
pineapples in abstract. Assemble this quilt to greet guests to your home year-round.*

Finished size 58-3/4×82-1/4"
35—11-3/4" square finished blocks

Select the fabric

1/2 yard each of
10 assorted mediums and darks

6 yards light prints for background

5/8 yard for binding

4 yards for backing

Cut the fabrics

1. From assorted mediums and darks, cut
   5—2-5/8" strips; from the strips cut
   70—2-5/8" squares (for a total of
   700—2-5/8" squares).

   1—7-1/2×14" rectangle (for a total of
   10—7-1/2×14" rectangles).

2. From light print, cut
   4—7-1/2" strips; from the strips, cut
   10 (total) 14" rectangles.

   24—4-3/4" strips. From 5 strips, cut
   35—4-3/4" squares;
   from 19 strips, cut
   280—2-5/8" rectangles.

   8—4-1/4" strips; from the strips, cut
   70—4-1/4" squares. Cut each square
   diagonally twice (in an X) to make
   280 setting triangles.

   7—3-7/8" strips; from the strips, cut
   70—3-7/8" squares. Cut each square
   diagonally once to make
   140 corner triangles.

3. From fabric for binding, cut
   7—2-1/2" strips; sew the strips end to
   end for a continuous length.

Build the Homestead Hospitality Blocks

1. Make 35 Unit A Center Squares.
   Right sides together, place 2—2-5/8"
   squares in different colors on opposite
   corners of a light print 4-3/4" square.
   Draw a diagonal line from corner to
   corner on each color square. Sew on
   both lines. Trim seams of color squares
   only. To set the seams, press flat before
   opening. Open out the triangles to
   the right side; press. Repeat to sew
   2—2-5/8" squares in different colors
   to opposite corners.

2. Make 280 Unit B Flying Geese, using
   2— 2-5/8" color squares on each
   2-5/8×4-3/4" rectangle. Right sides
   together, align a square along one side
   of each rectangle. Draw a line from
   corner to outside corner. Sew on the
   line, trim the seam, and turn the
   triangle to the right side. Repeat to
   sew the opposite side for each Flying
   Geese unit.

3. Make 140 Unit C triangle squares. Right sides together, align a light print 7-1/2×14" rectangle with each dark and medium print 7-1/2×14" rectangle. Press the rectangles together. Grid 8—3-1/4" squares on the wrong side of each light print. Draw a diagonal line through each square. Sew 1/4" on both sides of drawn line.

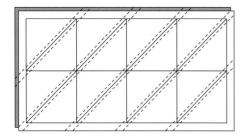

Cut on all the drawn lines, removing stitching from points. Press to set the seam; open the square; press seam toward darker fabric.

Square each unit to 2-5/8" with a quilter's square.

4. Make 140 of Unit D by sewing together 2 Unit B Flying Geese and 1 light background triangle.

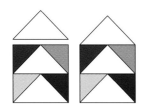

5. Sew a Unit D to a Unit A (Center Square) to make 35 of Unit E.

6. Noting placement, sew a setting triangle to each side of a 2-5/8" Triangle Square to make 140 of Unit F.

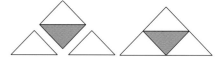

7. Sew a Unit F to each side of a Unit D, noting placement, to make 70 of Unit G.

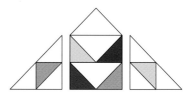

8. Sew a Unit G to each long side of a Unit E.

9. Press the blocks. Trim off the dog-ear points with a rotary cutter or scissors, leaving a 1/4" seam allowance all around for joining blocks together.

Assemble the rows

1. Lay out the blocks in 7 rows of 5 blocks each.

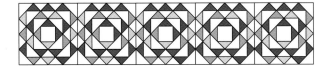

2. Sew each row of blocks together. Press the seams of adjacent rows in opposite directions.

3. Join the rows of blocks, butting seams for crisp points. Press the seams flat.

Finish the quilt

Refer to General Instructions, *pages 9–15,* to layer, baste, quilt, and bind the quilt.

Row Assembly

Homestead Hospitality Finished Quilt Assembly

Rail Fence

A township of houses, surrounded by rustic rails, will get conversation flowing about the neighborliness of rural living throughout our grand country.

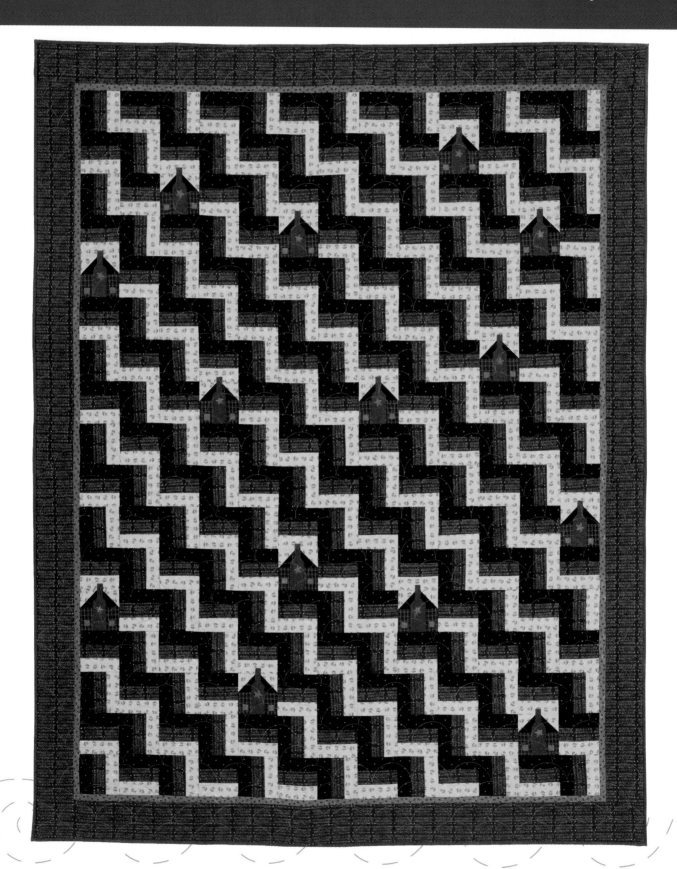

Select fabric and materials

1-2/3 yards black with stars for blocks

3 yards red print for blocks and outer border

1-7/8 yards beige print for blocks

1/4 yard red plaid for houses

1/4 yard dark for roofs

1/8 yard blue for chimney

1/2 yard gold for windows, stars, and inner border

2/3 yard for binding

4-1/2 yards for backing

Fusible webbing

Template plastic

Cut the fabric

1. From black with stars print, cut 26—2" strips.

2. From red print, cut 26—2" strips.

    8—5" strips. Sew the strips for a continuous length.

3. From beige print, cut 26—2" strips.

    2—2-1/2" strips; from the strips, cut 28—2-1/2" squares.

4. From red plaid for houses, cut 2—3" strips.

5. From dark for roofs, cut 2—2-1/2" strips.

6. From gold, cut 8—1-1/4" strips for the inner border. Sew the strips end to end for a continuous length; from the length cut
    2—60-1/2" top and bottom lengths
    2—77" side lengths.

7. For binding, cut 8—2-1/2" strips; sew the strips end to end for a continuous length.

Chimney, Stars, and Windows

1. Following manufacturer's directions, adhere fusible adhesive material to the wrong side of the blue fabric for the chimney and the gold fabric for the stars and windows, leaving the paper intact.

2. Trace the chimney, star, and window patterns, *page 121*, onto template plastic.

3. Trace the templates onto the paper side of fusible adhesive to make 14 chimneys, 14 stars, and 28 windows. Cut out the shapes on the traced lines. Set aside.

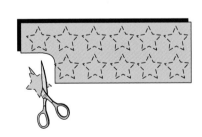

Make 207 Rail blocks

1. Sew together 1 each black, red, and beige 2" strips to make 26 strip sets. Press seams toward the darker fabrics. The strip width should measure 5".

2. From the strip sets, cut 207—5" segments.

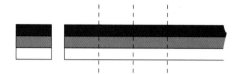

Make 14 House blocks

1. Sew each 3" red plaid strip to a 2-1/2" black strip for 2 strip sets. Press seams toward the darker fabric. Strip widths should measure 5".

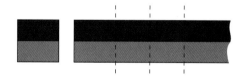

2. From the strips, cut 14—5" segments.

3. Right sides together, use template-free-angle piecing to sew a 2-1/2" beige print square to each side of the roof on the 5" segments. Press to set the seams, trim, and open out the triangles. Press.

4. Align a 5" square Rail segment and a 5" square House segment right sides together along the beige prints. Sew the segments together to make 14 House blocks. Press.

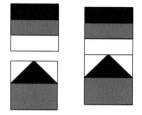

5. Position a chimney on each House block. Fuse the fabrics according to fusing material instructions. If desired, appliqué the chimney to the block by hand or machine. Place the star and windows on the House block, fuse, and appliqué as desired.

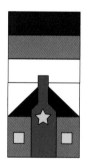

Assemble the Rows

1. Lay out the Rail and House Blocks in 13 vertical rows, staggering House Blocks throughout.

2. Join the blocks in rows; press seams in one direction, alternating direction for adjacent rows.

3. Sew the rows together. Press the seams in one direction. Stitch close to the quilt edge all around.

Sew on the borders

1. Sew a gold 77" inner border strip to each side of the quilt top. Press seams toward the border. Sew 60-1/2" inner border strips to the top and bottom of the quilt top. Press.

2. Measure the quilt top lengthwise through the center. Cut 5" outer borders to fit the sides. Sew the lengths to each side. Press seams toward the outer borders.

3. Measure the quilt top widthwise through the center. Cut 5" outer borders to fit the top and bottom. Sew the lengths to the top and bottom. Press seams toward the outer borders.

Finish the quilt

Refer to General Instructions, *pages 9–15*, to layer, baste, quilt, and bind the quilt.

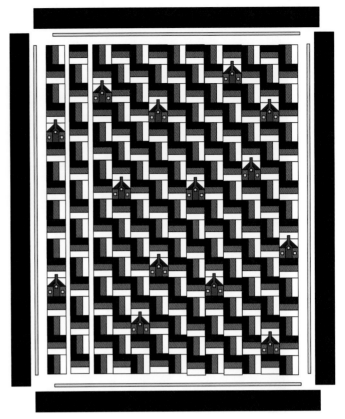

Row and Border Assembly

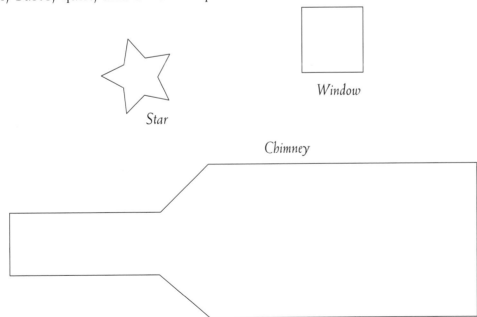

Star

Window

Chimney

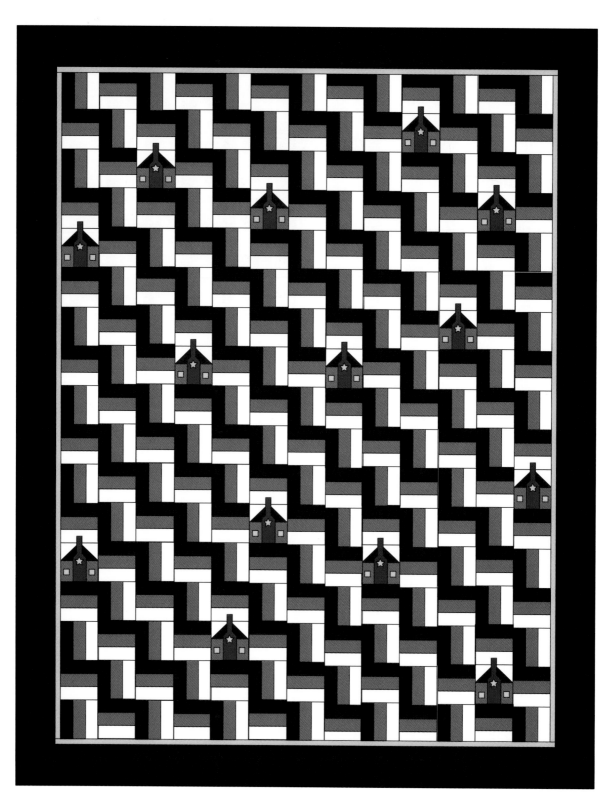

Rail Fence Finished Quilt Assembly

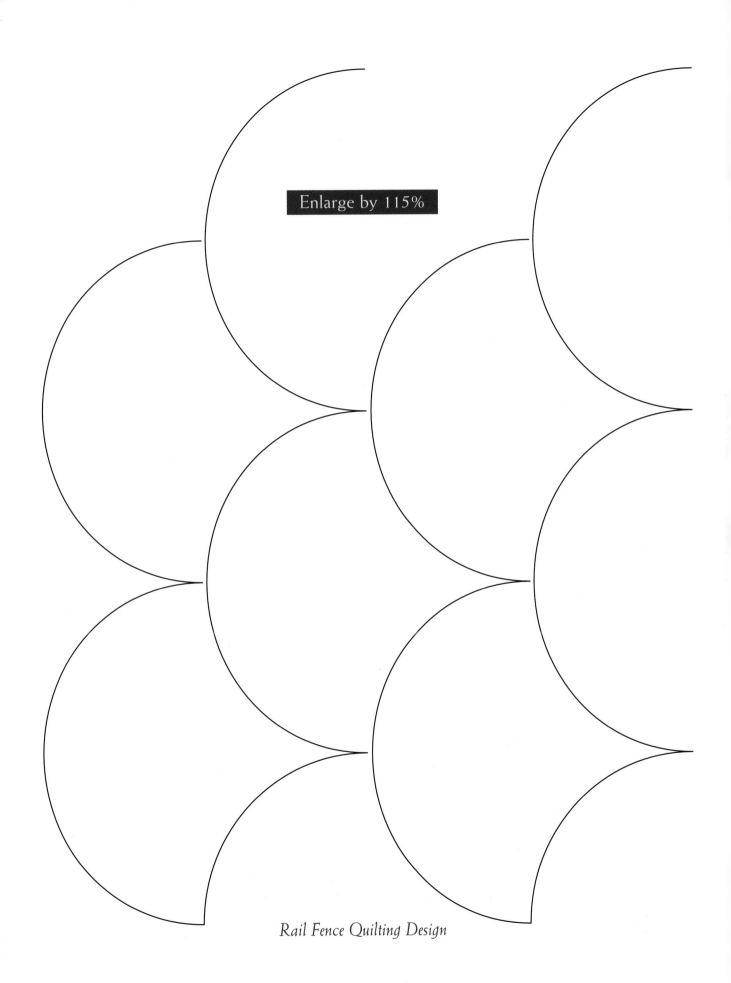

Enlarge by 115%

Rail Fence Quilting Design

Pineapple Plantation

Welcome symbols are always in season. Stitch and appliqué this contemporary pineapple version to convey heartfelt hospitality within your home.

Finished size 41×53-3/4"

Select fabric and materials

3/4 yard gold

2-1/4 yards off-white print

1 yard red print

5/8 yard light green

1/8 yard dark green

1-5/8 yards backing

Lightweight fusible webbing adhesive

Template plastic

Tri-Recs™ Tool set from EZ Quilting

Cut the fabric

1. From gold, cut
    3—2-1/2" strips; from the strips, cut
    63—2-1/2" Tri Tool Triangles.

    4—1-1/4" strips for the inner accent
    border; from the strips cut
    2—43-3/4" strips for sides and
    2—32-1/2" strips for top and bottom.

2. From off-white print, cut
    12—2-1/2" strips; from the strips, cut
    126—2-1/2" Recs Tool Triangles and
    36—1-1/2×2-1/2" rectangles.

    5—1-1/4" strip; from the strips, cut
    18—6-1/2" rectangles and
    9—8" rectangles.

    2—8" strips; from the strips, cut
    9—5-1/2" rectangles.

5—5" strips for outer border. Sew
strips end to end for a continuous
length. From the length, cut
2—45-1/4" side lengths and
2—41-1/2" top and bottom lengths.

3. From red print, cut
    8—2-1/2" strips. From 4 of the strips,
    cut 12—12-1/4" rectangles; from
    4 of the strips, cut 4—31" rectangles.

    5—2-1/2" strips; sew the strips end to
    end for a continuous binding length.

Make 9 Pineapple Plantation Blocks

1. Using the gold triangles and the
    off-white print half rectangles,
    assemble 63 pineapple triangles,
    following the Tri-Recs instructions.

2. Assemble 18 units of
    2 Pineapple triangles
    and 2—1-1/2×2-1/2"
    background rectangles
    each. Press seams away
    from the gold points.

3. Assemble 9 units of
    3 Pineapple triangles.
    Press the seams toward
    the gold points.

4. Right sides together, sew
    a 2-Pineapple unit to each long side
    of a 3-Pineapple unit. Press seams in
    one direction.

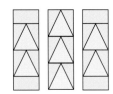

5. Sew a 1-1/4×6-1/2" rectangle to both sides of each Pineapple block. Press seams toward the off-white rectangle. Sew a 1-1/4×8" rectangle to the bottom of the Pineapple block; press the seam toward the off-white rectangle.

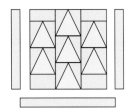

6. Sew a 5-1/2×8" off-white rectangle to the top of each Pineapple block. Press the seams toward the off-white fabric.

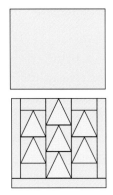

Assemble Pineapple blocks with sashing strips

1. Lay out the blocks in 3 rows of 3 blocks each.

2. Sew 4 red print 2-1/2×12-1/4" sashing strips between the blocks and to border the blocks for each row. Press the seams toward the red sashing.

3. Sew a red print 2-1/2×31" sashing strip along the top row and the bottom row. Press seams toward the red sashing.

Sew on the borders

1. Sew the gold 1-1/4" accent border

strips first to the sides then to the top and bottom of the quilt top. Press the seams toward the red sashing.

2. Sew the off-white 5" outer borders strips first to the sides then to the top and bottom of the quilt top. Press the seams toward the gold accent borders.

Row and Border Assembly

Appliqué the Pineapple top, vine, leaves, and stars

1. **Note:** *If hand-appliquéing, add 1/4" to leaf, star, and vine templates.* Follow fusible webbing adhesive manufacturer's directions and General Instructions, *pages 12–13,* to apply webbing to the

wrong side of gold, light green, and dark green fabrics.

2. Trace the Pineapple top, vine, leaf, and star patterns, *pages 128–129*, to template plastic. Trace the templates to the paper side of fusible webbing.

3. Cut out the shapes on the traced lines and fuse them to the quilt top.

4. Appliqué the shapes by hand or machine, using matching threads.

Finish the quilt

Refer to General Instructions, *pages 9–15*, to layer, baste, quilt, and bind the quilt.

Pineapple Plantation Finished Quilt Assembly

Pineapple Plantation Patterns

*For hand-appliqué, cut templates 1/4"
larger all around.*

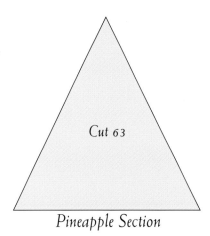

Pineapple Section

Cut 63

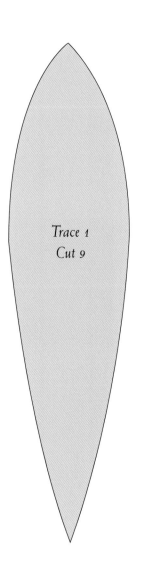

*Trace 1
Cut 9*

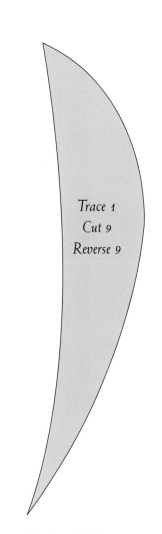

*Trace 1
Cut 9
Reverse 9*

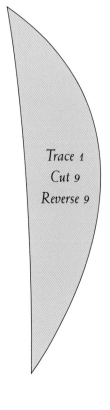

*Trace 1
Cut 9
Reverse 9*

Pineapple Top

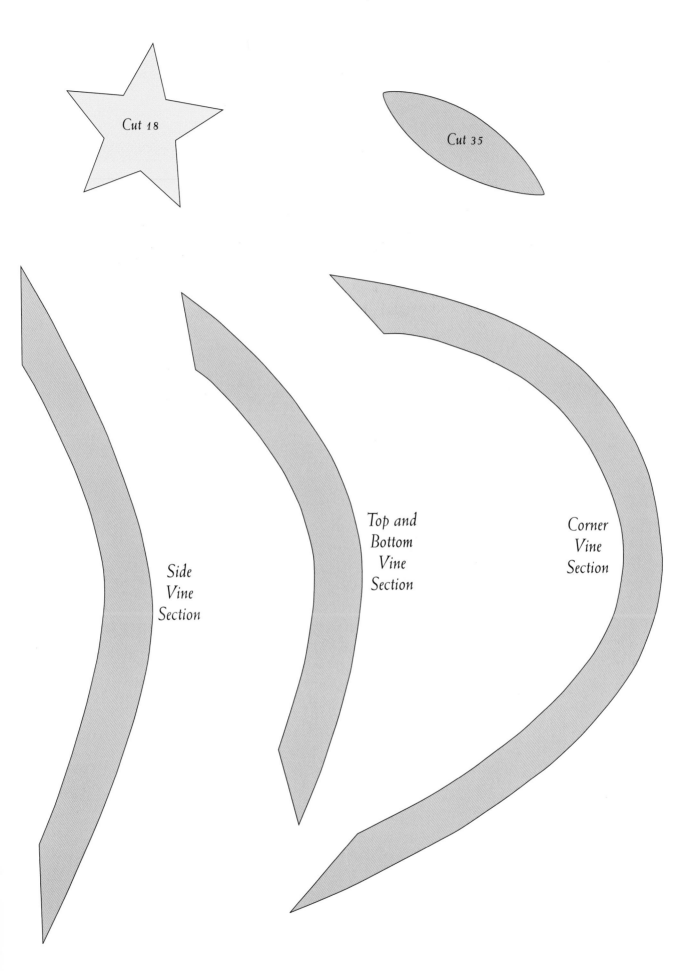

Cut 18

Cut 35

Side
Vine
Section

Top and
Bottom
Vine
Section

Corner
Vine
Section

Pineapple Plantation Quilting Design

Pineapple Plantation Sashing Quilting Design

Welcome Home Log Cabin

Traditional sometimes takes an upbeat turn. Create a distinct version of your own by using color families for quiet refinement or sharp contrasts for vivid impact.

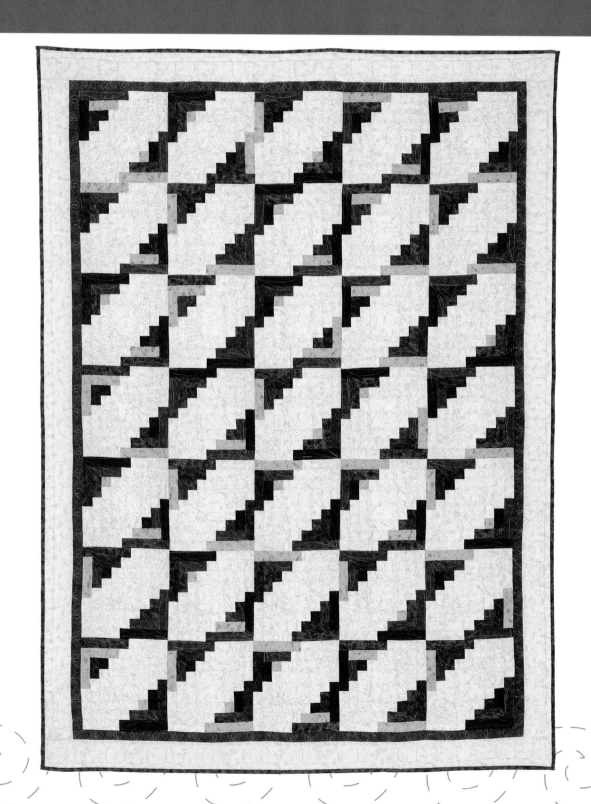

Finished size 55×73"
35—9" finished blocks

Select the fabric

5 yards light for background, outer border, and binding

1/2 yard each of 5 assorted darks

3/8 yard red solid for inner border

3-3/4 yards for backing

Cut the fabric

1. From light, cut
   7—2-1/2" strips; sew the strips end to end for a continuous binding length.

   19—3-1/2" strips. Set aside 10 strips. From 9 strips, cut and label the following sizes:
   > 35—3-1/2" squares (#1)
   > 35—1-1/2" rectangles (#2)
   > 35—4-1/2" rectangles (#4).

   7—4" strips for the outer border. Sew the strips end to end for a continuous length. From the length, cut
   2—65-1/2" side lengths and
   2—54-1/2" top and bottom lengths.

   10—4-1/2" strips.

2. From assorted darks, cut
   4—1-1/2" strips
   4—2-1/2" strips
   4—3-1/2" strips
   4—4-1/2" strips
   4—5-1/2" strips.

3. From red solid, cut
   6—1-1/2" strips; sew the strips end to end for a continuous length. Cut
   2—63-1/2" side lengths and
   2—47-1/2" top and bottom lengths.

Make 10 strip sets

1. Using 1 light and one dark, sew together **2 each** of the following widths to make 20 strip sets:

Strip Sets #3:
1-1/2" dark and
3-1/2" light

Strip Set #3

Strip Sets #5:
4-1/2" light and
1-1/2" dark

Strip Set #5

Strip Sets #6:
2-1/2" dark and
3-1/2" light

Strip Set #6

Strip Sets #7:
3-1/2" dark and
3-1/2" light

Strip Set #7

Strip Sets #8:
2-1/2" dark and
4-1/2" light

Strip Set #8

Strip Sets #9:
4-1/2" light and
3-1/2" dark

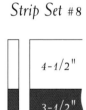

Strip Set #9

Strip Sets #10:
4-1/2" dark and
3-1/2" light

Strip Set #10

Strip Sets #11:
5-1/2" dark and
3-1/2" light

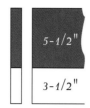

5-1/2"

3-1/2"

Strip Set #11

Strip Sets #12:
4-1/2" dark and
4-1/2" light

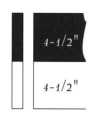

4-1/2"

4-1/2"

Strip Set #12

Strip Sets #13:
4-1/2" light and
5-1/2" dark

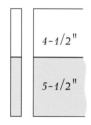

4-1/2"

5-1/2"

Strip Set #13

Press seams toward the dark fabric. From each strip set, cut 35—1-1/2" segments, separating and labeling each size for identification in assembling the blocks.

Make 35—9-1/2" Log Cabin blocks

1. Using the chain sewing method, (See General Instructions, *page 13*), sew a #2—1-1/2×3-1/2" rectangle to one side of each #1—3-1/2 square. Press seams toward the rectangle.

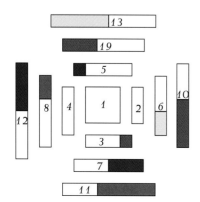

2. Sew consecutive strips clockwise, numerically, to the unit. Press seams toward the outer rectangle after each addition.

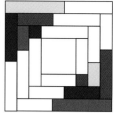

Assemble rows and borders

1. Lay out 7 rows of 5 Log Cabin blocks each. Sew each row together. Press block seams in each row in the opposite direction from adjacent rows.

2. Sew rows together, butting block seams. Press seams in one direction.

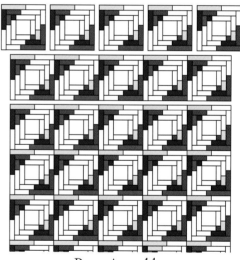

Row Assembly

3. Sew a red 63-1/2" length to each side of the quilt top; press seams toward the border. Sew a red 47-1/2" length to the top and bottom of the quilt top; press seams toward the border.

4. Sew a light 65-1/2" outer border length to each side of the quilt top; press seams toward the red border. Sew a light 54-1/2" length to the top and bottom; press seams toward the red border.

Finish the quilt

Refer to General Instructions, *pages 9–15*, to layer, baste, quilt, and bind the quilt.

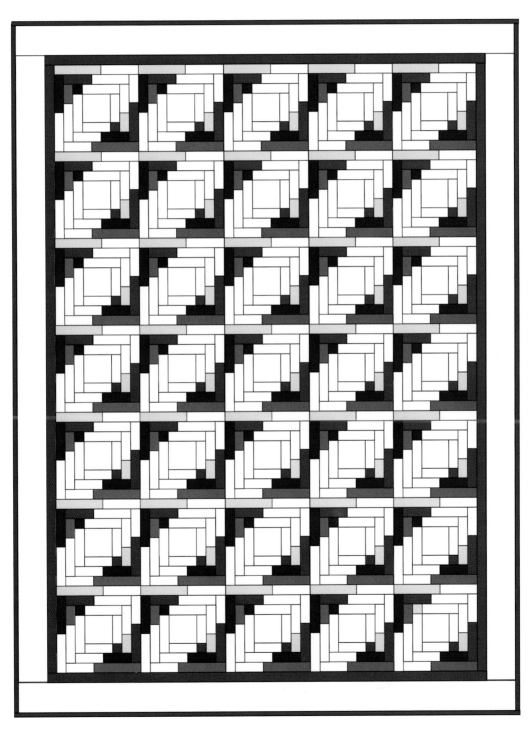

Welcome Home Log Cabin Finished Quilt Assembly

Welcome Home Log Cabin Quilting Design

Finished size 86-1/2" square

Select the fabric

6-1/4 yards light print
for background and border

4 yards medium blue print for
blocks and binding

6 yards for backing

Cut the fabrics

1. From light, cut
   36—2" strips
   12—5" strips; from the strips, cut
   96—5" squares.

   3—7-3/4" strips; from the strips, cut
   11—7 3/4" squares. Cut each square
   diagonally twice (in an X) for
   44 setting triangles.

   From a portion of the remaining 7-3/4"
   strip, cut 2—4-1/4" squares; cut the
   squares diagonally once for
   4 corner triangles.

   9—5-1/2" strips for the border.
   Sew the strips end to end for a
   continuous length.

2. From blue, cut
   33—2" strips. From 15 of the strips,
   cut 288—2" squares

   4—5" strips; from the strips, cut
   25—5" squares

   9—2-1/2" strips; sew the strips end to
   end for a continuous binding length.

Sew 18 strip sets

1. Sew together 1 dark and 2 light
   2" strips to make 18 light-dark-light
   strip sets. Press seams toward the
   center dark strip. The width of the
   finished strip sets must measure 5".
   From the strip sets, cut
   144—5" segments.

Sew T-Blocks and 12 rows of units

1. Make 144 T-Blocks. Using template-
   free angle-
   piecing, sew
   2—2" blue
   squares to
   adjacent
   corners of
   one side of each 5" segment. Press
   seams toward the blue triangles.

2. Make 36 of Unit A: Sew a T-Block
   (T toward center) to opposite sides of
   36—5" light squares.

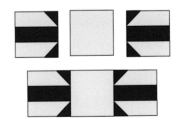

3. Make 30 of Unit B: Sew a T-Block
   (T upward) to one side of 30—5"
   light squares.

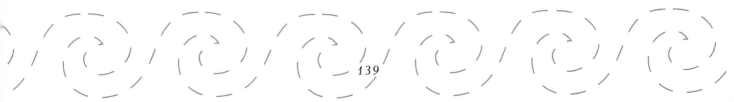

4. Make 30 of Unit C: Sew a T-Block (T downward) to one side of 30—5" light squares.

5. Sew Units B and C together with each T in opposite directions, a light square between them and a light square on the far right.

Assemble the rows

1. Assemble Rows 1 and 23 using 1 T-Block, 2 setting triangles and 1 corner triangle for each row.

2. Assemble Rows 2, and 22 using Unit A and setting triangles.

3. Assemble Rows 3, 5, 7, 9, 11, 13, 15, 17, 19, and 21 with the joined Units B and C; sew a T-Block to one end of each row. Sew setting triangles to the row ends.

4. Assemble Rows 4, 6, 8, 10, 12, 14, 16, 18, and 20 with Unit A and the 5" blue squares. Sew setting triangles to the row ends.

5. Lay out the rows.

6. Sew together Rows 1 through 11; then Rows 13 through 23 to make two halves. Sew Row 12 to one half; join the two halves. Press the seams flat.

7. Lay the quilt top flat. Use a rotary ruler to trim off seam points, allowing 1/4" seam allowance evenly around the quilt top.

Sew on the border

1. Measure the length of the quilt top through the center. From the light 5-1/2" outer border continuous length, cut 2 lengths to fit. Sew one to each side of the quilt top. Press seams toward the outer border.

2. Measure the width of the quilt top through the center. Cut 2 outer border lengths to measurement; sew one to the top and one to the bottom of the quilt top. Press seams toward the outer border.

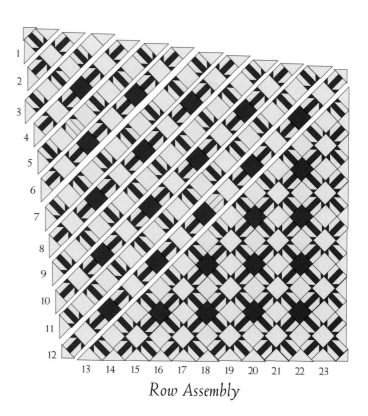

Row Assembly

Finish the quilt

Refer to General Instructions, *pages 9–15,* to layer, baste, quilt, and bind the quilt.

Indigo Finished Quilt Assembly

Morning Glory

Dresden Plate and Fan patterns, printed in women's magazines of the '20s and '30s, became popular for piecing colorful fabric scraps. From necessity grows beauty.

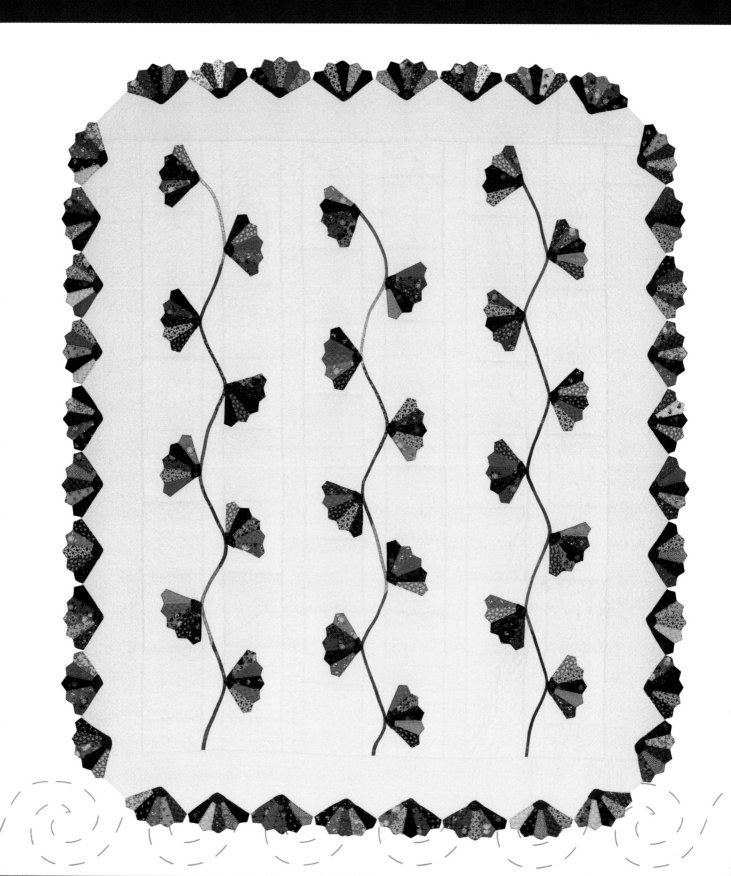

Finished size 79×100"

Select fabric and materials

7 yards white or off-white

17 assorted color fat-quarters (18×22")

3 yards muslin (flower and sepal facing)

6 assorted green fat-quarters

6 yards for backing

1/2" bias tape maker

Perlé cotton in contrasting colors

Template plastic

Cut the fabric

1. From white or off-white, cut
    21—8-1/2" strips; from 12 strips, cut
    48—10" rectangles. From 1 strip, cut
    6—4-1/2" rectangles.

    Sew the remaining strips together, end
    to end, in pairs. From the lengths, cut
    2—80-1/2" lengths and
    2—79-1/2" lengths.

    10—3-1/2" strips. Sew the strips
    together in pairs. From the pairs, cut
    5—80-1/2" lengths.

2. From muslin, cut 15—6" strips; cut
    each strip into quarters (approximately
    11") to face each joined flower petal
    unit. Use the remaining muslin to face
    the sepals.

Cut and sew 60 Morning Glories

1. Trace the Morning Glory petal,
    page 155, to template plastic; cut out
    the template.

2. Trace 18 Morning Glory petals onto
    the wrong side of each fat quarter,
    spacing petals 1/2" apart. Cut out the
    petals on the traced lines.

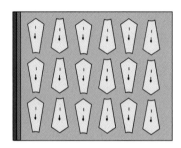

*Tip: To speed cutting, layer 2 or 3 fat quarters
facedown; press. Secure the layers with pins or
basting thread. Trace petals
onto the top fabric. Carefully cut through
the layers to cut out the petals. Use 300 of
the 306 petals.*

3. Arrange each flower using an
    assortment of 5 colors. Sew the petals
    together with a 1/4" seam. Press the
    seams in one direction.

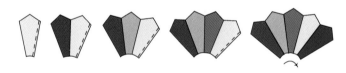

4. Right sides together, lay each flower
    on a piece of muslin. Stitch around the

long sides and points with a 1/4" seam, leaving an opening for turning along the curved center. Clip the seams at the inside of the points. Trim away excess muslin facing. Turn the flower unit right side out. Press, rolling the edges slightly toward the facing for a smooth finish.

Make bias-fold Vines and 60 Sepals

1. Fold each green fat quarter along the bias; press and slightly trim off the fold. Cut 2—1" bias strips from each fat quarter. Right sides together, sew the strips together end to end for 1 continuous length; press the seams open. Use a bias tape maker to make the bias folds; or press each strip in half lengthwise and fold the long edges in toward (*but not to*) the fold. Press the bias strip without stretching or distorting the tape by laying the iron on the fabric rather than sliding the iron across the fabric.

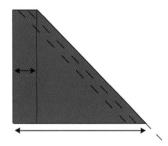

2. Trace the Sepal pattern onto template plastic. Cut out the template along the line.

3. Right sides together, layer remaining green fat-quarter fabric with a muslin piece. Trace the Sepal template to the wrong side of the muslin, spacing sepals approximately 1/2" apart. Pin layers together and cut out on the traced lines. Sew around each sepal

1/8" from the edge. Cut a small slit in the muslin facing, turn to the right side, and press, rolling the seam toward the muslin facing for a smooth finish.

Assemble blocks and rows

1. Position a Morning Glory on each of 24—8-1/2×10" background rectangles, placing the flower center approximately 1/2" from a long edge and tilting the flowers slightly. Use perlé cotton and a running stitch to sew the flower to the background.

2. Lay out Morning Glory blocks alternating with 8-1/2×10" background rectangles and placing 8-1/2×4-1/2" background rectangles along the bottom of 4 rows and the top of 2 rows. Sew the blocks together to make 6 vertical rows. Press the seams in one direction.

3. Noting flower placement, sew a 3-1/2×80-1/2" background strip between each 2-row set. Press the seams toward the center strip. Position and topstitch the bias strip vines using perlé cotton and a running stitch. Stitch the sepals in place with pearl cotton.

4. Sew a 3-1/2×80-1/2" strip to each long side of the center row set. Sew the outer rows to each long side of the center. Press seams toward the narrow background strips.

Sew on the borders and Morning Glory edging

1. Sew a 8-1/2×80-1/2" background strip to each long side for borders. Press seams toward the borders. Sew a 8-1/2×79-1/2" background strip to the top and to the bottom of the quilt top for borders. Press seams toward the borders.

2. Along the outer borders, measure and mark 6-3/4" from each corner. Align the two marks with a ruler. Draw a line to connect the marks and cut along the line with scissors or align a ruler and cut with a rotary cutter to connect the marks.

Finish the quilt

1. Refer to General Instructions, *pages 9–15*, to layer, baste, quilt, and bind the quilt.

2. Position remaining Morning Glories around the edges of the quilt top. Use perlé cotton to handstitch the flowers in place.

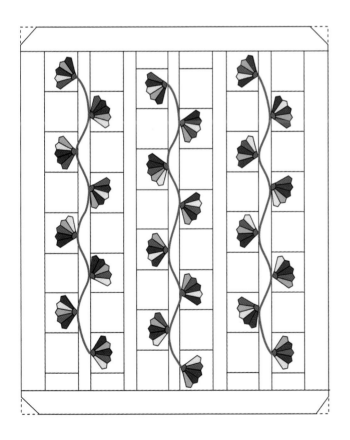

Row and Border Assembly

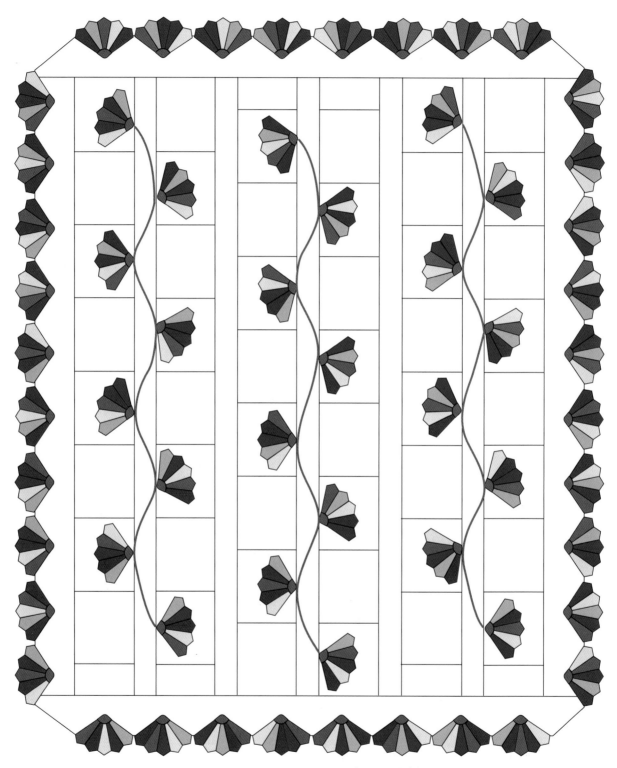

Morning Glory Finished Quilt Assembly

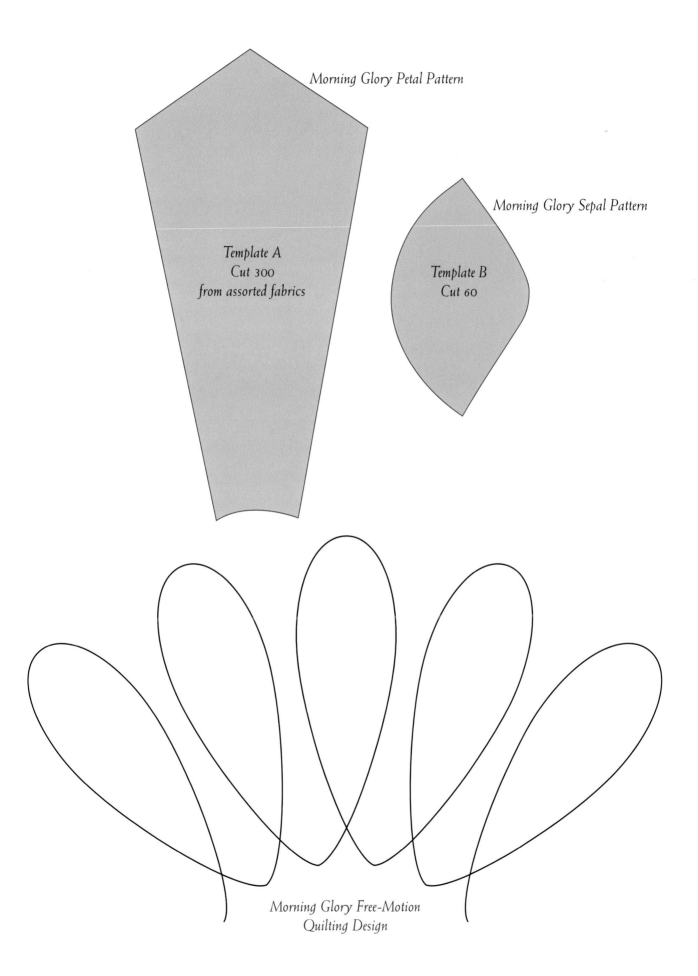

Morning Glory Petal Pattern

Morning Glory Sepal Pattern

Template A
Cut 300
from assorted fabrics

Template B
Cut 60

Morning Glory Free-Motion
Quilting Design

149

Morning Glory Quilting Design

Morning Glory Quilting Design

Raised Beds

Resembling flower beds amid surrounding walkways, these neatly arranged squares within squares bloom with myriad hues of red and pink roses and carnations.

Finished size 53×68"

Select the fabric

*2 yards light floral background print
for blocks, block borders,
and second inner border*

*1/4 yard each of 4 assorted medium pink
floral prints (or 1/8 yard each of
8 assorted medium floral prints)*

*1/4 yard each of 5 assorted
dark pink floral prints*

*1-1/2 yards red print for sashing,
first inner border, and outer border*

3-1/2 yards for backing

Cut the fabric

1. From light floral background print, cut

    6—2-1/2" strips; sew the strips end
    to end for a continuous length to use
    for binding.

    8—2" strips

    22—1-1/8" strips; from 16 strips, cut
    24—12-1/2" rectangles and
    24—13-3/4" rectangles to frame the
    blocks. Sew the remaining 6—1-1/8"
    strip lengths end to end for continuous
    length. From the length, cut
    2—62-1/4" and
    2—48-1/2" inner border lengths.

2. From each of 4 medium pinks, cut
    2—2" strips for blocks (or from each
    of 8 medium, cut 1—2" strip).

3. From each of 5 dark pinks,
    2—3-1/2" strips; from the strips, cut
    20—3-1/2" squares from each print for
    a total of 100—3-1/2" squares.

4. From red print, cut

    6—2-3/4" strips; sew the strips
    together end to end for a continuous
    length; from the length, cut
    2—63-1/2" side and
    2—53" top and bottom lengths.

    11—2-1/4" strips. From 3 strips, cut
    8—13-3/4" short sashing lengths. Sew
    the remaining 2-1/4" strips together
    end to end for a continuous length;
    from the length, cut
    3—43-3/4" sashing lengths,
    2—58-3/4" inner border side and
    2—47-1/4" inner border top and
    bottom lengths.

Make 12 Raised Bed blocks

1. Sew each 2" light floral print strip to a
    2" assorted medium pink floral print
    strip, right sides together along the
    long edges, to make 8 strip sets. Press
    seams toward the pink fabric. From the
    strip sets, cut 192—2" segments.

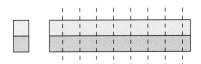

2. Sew pairs of segments together,
    mixing prints and reversing
    light/medium positions to make
    96 Four-Patch blocks. Press seams in
    one direction.

3. Sew a 3-1/2" dark pink print square to each Four-Patch, positioning Four Patches in the same direction. Press seams toward the 3-1/2" square.

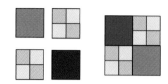

4. Join the units to make 12 blocks; press seams toward the darker fabrics.

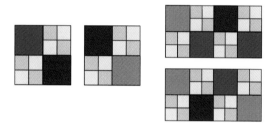

Assemble blocks with sashing and borders

1. Sew 1-1/8×12-1/2" light floral background strips to opposite sides of each block, noting color position. Press seams toward the strip. Sew 1-1/8×13-3/4" light floral background strips to the top and bottom. Press seams toward the strips.

2. Lay out the blocks in 4 rows of 3 blocks, placing blocks with the same orientation of light and dark blocks.

3. Sew a 2-1/4×13-3/4" sashing strip to sides of each center block. Sew adjacent blocks to sashing to make a row. Press seams toward sashing strips.

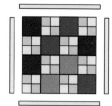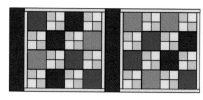

4. Sew long 2-1/4×43-3/4" sashing strips to join Rows 1 and 2 and Rows 3 and 4. Press seams toward sashing.

5. Sew a 58-3/4" red print inner border strip to each side of the quilt top. Press. Sew a 47-1/4" red print inner border strip to the top and bottom of the quilt top. Press.

6. Sew a narrow 62-1/4" light floral background print inner accent strip to each side of the quilt top; press. Sew a narrow 48-1/2" light floral background print inner accent strip to the top and bottom of the quilt top; press.

7. Sew red print 63-1/2" outer border strips to each side of the quilt top; press the seams. Sew a red print 53" outer border strip to the top and to the bottom of the quilt top; press.

Finish the quilt

Refer to General Instructions, *pages 9–15*, to layer, baste, quilt, and bind the quilt.

Raised Beds Finished Quilt Assembly

Raised Beds
Quilting Design

Raised Beds
Free-Motion Quilting Design

Rosemary

Feathery texture and mellow hues come through on this two-tone summery quilt that pays tribute to the popular, fragrant herb that flavors food and the senses.

Finished size 71-3/4×79-1/4"

Select the fabric

5-1/2 yards light print

11 assorted fat-quarters (18×22")

5 yards for backing

Cut the fabric

1. From light print, cut
    61—1-3/4" strips; from the strips, cut
    121—20" lengths.

    8—4-1/4" strips; from the strips, cut
    72—4-1/4" squares.

    7—1-3/4" strips; sew the strips end to
    end for a continuous length.

    8—2" strips; sew the strips end to end
    for a continuous length.

2. From each assorted fat-quarter, cut
    8—1-3/4" strips (for a total of
    88—1-3/4×20" strips)

    38—1-3/4×4-1/4" rectangles from
    assorted fat-quarters.

Piece blocks from the strip sets

1. Sew an assorted 1-3/4" strip to each
    long side of the 17 light print 1-3/4"
    strips to make 17 Unit A Strip Sets.
    Press the seams toward the darker
    fabric in the strip set. From the strip
    sets, cut 180—1-3/4" segments.

2. Sew a light print 1-3/4" strip to each
    long side of 12 assorted 1-3/4" strips
    to make 12 Unit B Strip Sets. Press the
    seams toward the darker fabric in each
    strip set. From the strip sets, cut
    128—1-3/4" segments.

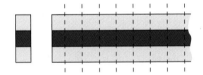

3. Sew a Unit A segment to each long
    side of a Unit B segment to make
    90 Nine-Patch blocks. Press seams
    toward the Unit A segments.

4. Sew a light 1-3/4" strip to each long
    side of 40 assorted 1-3/4" strips to
    make 40 Unit C Strip Sets. Press
    seams toward the darker fabric.
    From the strip sets, cut 161—4-1/4"
    Rail Block segments.

Assemble the rows

1. Sew together 9 Nine-Patches and 8 Rail Blocks to make 10 rows. Press seams toward the Rail Blocks.

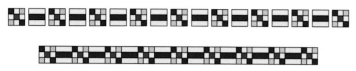

2. Sew together 9 Rail Blocks and 8 light 4-1/4" squares to make 9 rows. Press seams toward the Rail Blocks.

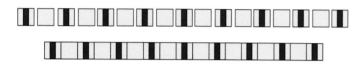

3. Sew together the rows, beginning and ending with Nine Patch rows. Press seams toward the Nine-Patch rows.

Sew on the borders

1. From the light 1-3/4" continuous length, cut 2—71-3/4" lengths. Sew a length to each side; press the seams toward the border strips.

2. Cut 2—66-3/4" lengths. Sew one to the top and one to the bottom. Press the seams toward the border strips.

3. Piece side border lengths from 10—1-3/4×4-1/4" assorted rectangles and 10—Unit B segments for each length. From one end of each length, remove one light square. Press seams in one direction. Sew a pieced border to each long side of the quilt top. Press seams toward the solid border.

4. Piece top and bottom border lengths from 9—1-3/4×4-1/4" assorted rectangles and 10—Unit B segments for each length. Repeat Step 3 to complete the border.

5. Measure the quilt top through the center to determine outer border side lengths. From the light 2" continuous strips, cut 2 lengths to fit; sew one to each side. Press seams toward the outer border.

6. Measure the quilt top to determine outer border top and bottom lengths. From the light 2" continuous strips, cut 2 lengths to fit; sew one to the top and one to the bottom. Press seams toward the outer border.

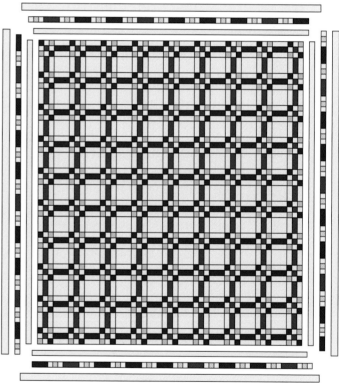

Row and Border Assembly

Finish the quilt

Refer to General Instructions, *pages 9–15*, to layer, baste, quilt, and bind the quilt.

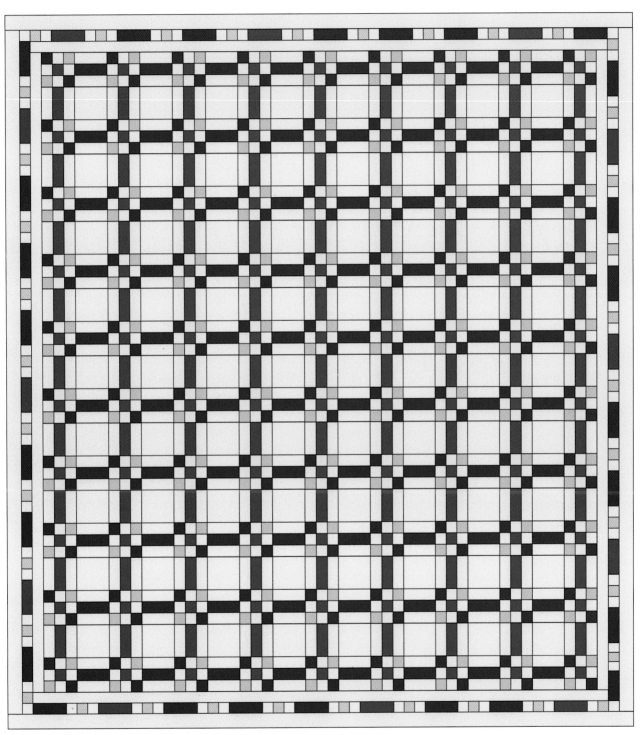

Rosemary Finished Quilt Assembly

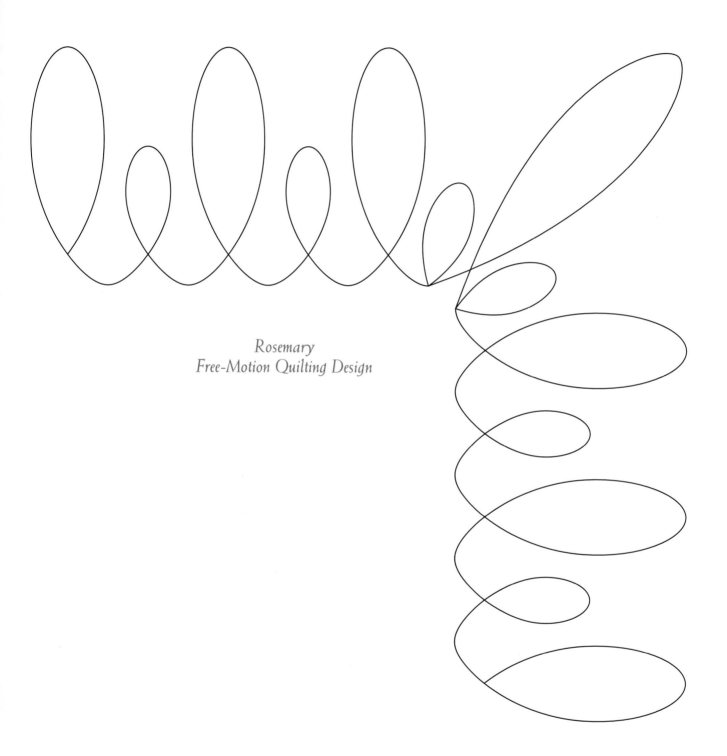

Rosemary
Free-Motion Quilting Design

Rosemary Quilting Design

Seed Packets

Who hasn't been inspired by luscious photos and drawings of endless garden possibilities on little packages of seeds—especially during cold indoor months?

Finished size 60×64"
63—4" finished blocks

Select the fabric

16 assorted fat-quarters
(18×22")

1-1/2 yards light print

3/4 yard dark print
for inner and outer borders

5/8 yard for binding

3-3/4 yards for backing

Cut the fabric

1. From assorted fat-quarters, cut
   3—1-1/2" strips
   1—12" square
   1—1-1/4" strip (for pieced border).

2. From light, cut
   7—4-1/2" strips; from the strips, cut
   126—2-1/8" rectangles.

3. From dark print, cut
   5—1-1/4" strips; sew the strips end to
   end for a continuous length. From the
   length, cut
   2—51-1/2" and
   2—41-1/2" inner border lengths.

   6—3-1/2" strips; sew the strips end to
   end for a continuous length. From the
   length, cut
   2—58-1/2" and
   2—60-1/2" outer border lengths.

4. From fabric for binding, cut
   6—2-1/2" strips; sew the strips end to
   end for a continuous length.

Assemble 63 Seed Packet blocks from strip sets and quarter-triangle squares

1. Sew together 4 assorted 1-1/2" fat-
   quarter strips to make 12 strip sets.
   Press seams in one direction. From the
   strip sets, cut 110—1-1/4" segments.

2. Sew a 2-1/8×4-1/2" light rectangle to
   each long side of 63—1-1/4"
   segments. Press seams toward the
   light rectangles. Each block should
   measure 4-1/2" square. Set aside
   remaining segments.

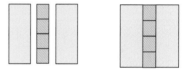

3. Right sides
   together, pair each
   12" square with a
   second 12" square.
   On the wrong side
   of the lighter square
   draw a grid of 4—
   5-3/4" squares.
   Draw an
   X on each
   square.

4. Sew 1/4" from
   one side of the
   diagonal lines
   (*do not stitch on*

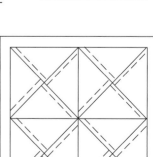

both sides of the diagonal lines). Cut on all the drawn lines. Press the half-square triangle units open; press seams toward the darker fabric.

5. Pair 96 assorted half-square triangle units to make 48 quarter-triangle squares, butting triangle seams in opposite directions for a smooth finish.

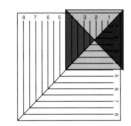

6. Square and trim each block to 4-1/2".

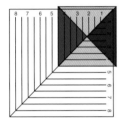

7. Trim 28 half-square triangle units (from Step 4 above) for setting triangles. With half-square triangle unit facing up, place the 45-degree angle of a square along the seam line. Trim the unit to 4-7/8" square.

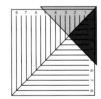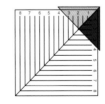

8. Unsew 2 half-square triangle units. Press them flat. Use a square to trim the 90 degree edges to 3-3/4" to make 4 corner triangles.

Join blocks in diagonal rows

1. Lay out the blocks in diagonal rows: 2 sets of Rows 1 through 7 and 1 of Row 8.

2. Sew the blocks together in each diagonal row, pressing seams toward the darker fabric.

3. Join the rows together, pressing seams in one direction. Sew all around the quilt top close to the edge.

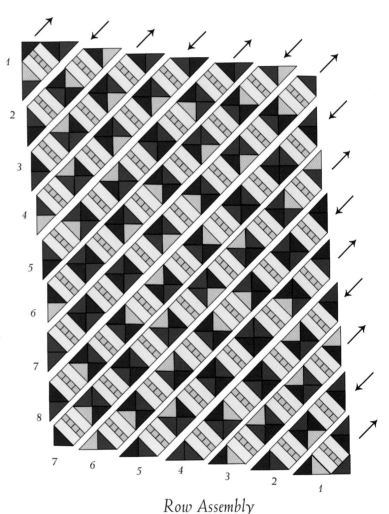

Row Assembly

Sew on the borders

1. Sew a 1-1/4×51-1/2" length to each side of the quilt top. Press seams toward the border. Sew 1-1/4×41-1/2" lengths to the top and bottom of the quilt top. Press seams toward the border.

2. Piece the remaining 1-1/4" segments together to make 2—52-1/2" side lengths and 2—42-1/2" top and bottom lengths.

3. Sew on the pieced side lengths; press seams toward the inner border. Sew on the pieced top and bottom lengths; press seams toward the inner border.

4. Measure the quilt top lengthwise through the center. From the continuous dark length, cut two strips to size and sew one to each side of the quilt. Press seams toward the borders.

5. Measure the quilt top widthwise through the center. Cut two dark inner border strips and sew one to the top and one to the bottom of the quilt. Press seams toward the borders.

Finish the quilt

Refer to General Instructions, *pages 9—15*, to layer, baste, quilt, and bind the quilt.

Border Assembly

Seed Packets Finished Quilt Assembly

Seed Packets Quilting Designs

Sweet Basil

Summer heat produces this aromatic herb. Use it to make pesto, to garnish salads, to flavor poultry, and to serve as inspiration to make a colorfully warm quilt.

Finished size 64×88"

Select the fabric

5 yards light for background

1-3/4 yards total assorted medium

1-1/4 yards dark

2/3 yard binding

5-3/4 yards backing

Cut the fabric

1. From light, cut
   21—4-1/2" strips; from the strips, cut
   82—8-1/2" rectangles.

   20—2-1/2" strips; from 5 of the strips,
   cut 70—2-1/2" squares.

   16—1-1/2" strips.

2. From assorted medium, cut
   32—1-1/2" strips.

3. From dark, cut 13—2 1/2" strips.

Piece 48—4" Nine-Patch blocks

1. Sew a 1-1/2" medium strip to each
   long side of 4—2-1/2" light strips to
   make 4 strip sets. Press seams toward
   the medium fabric. From the strip sets,
   cut 96—1-1/2" segments.

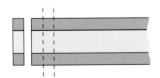

2. Sew a 1-1/2" light strip to each long
   side of 3—2-1/2" dark strips to make
   3 strip sets. Press seams toward the
   dark fabric. From the strip sets, cut
   48—2-1/2" segments.

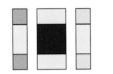

3. Right sides together, sew a 1-1/2"
   segment to each side of a 2-1/2"
   segment to complete 48 Nine-Patch
   blocks. Press seams toward the
   1-1/2" segments.

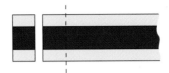

Piece 35 Sweet Basil blocks

1. Sew an assorted 1-1/2" medium strip
   to each long side of 6—2-1/2" light
   strips to make 6 strip sets. Press seams
   toward the medium strips. From the
   strip sets, cut 140—1-1/2" segments.

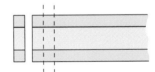

2. Sew 2—1-1/2" segments together to
   make 70—1-1/2×8-1/2" lengths. Press
   seams in one direction.

3. Sew a 2-1/2" dark strip to each long side of 5—2-1/2" light strips; sew a 1-1/2" light strip to each long outer edge of the dark strips to make 5 strip sets. Press seams toward the dark strips. From the strip sets, cut 70—2-1/2" segments.

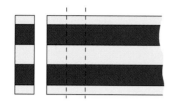

4. Sew together 2 assorted 1-1/2" medium strips to make 6 strip sets. Press seams in one direction. From the strip sets, cut 140—1-1/2" segments.

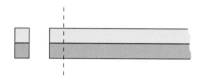

5. Join 70 of the 1-1/2" segments in pairs to make 35 Four-Patch blocks.

6. Sew together 2—1-1/2" medium segments, 2—2-1/2" light squares, and a Four-Patch in the order shown to make 35 center block units. Press seams toward the darker fabric.

7. Sew together 2—1-1/2"×8-1/2" lengths, 2—2-1/2" segments, and the center block unit to make 35 Sweet Basil blocks. Press seams.

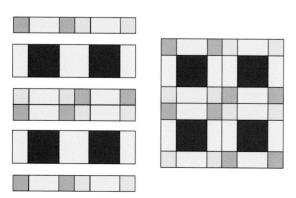

Assemble the rows

1. Lay out the blocks with the 4-1/2×8-1/2" light rectangles to make 8 rows of Nine-Patch blocks and 7 rows of Sweet Basil blocks.

2. Join the blocks in rows by sewing rectangles to the sides. Press seams toward the Nine-Patch blocks and Sweet Basil blocks.

3. Join the rows in pairs, sewing each Nine-Patch row to a Sweet Basil row. Sew the pairs of rows together. Press the seams.

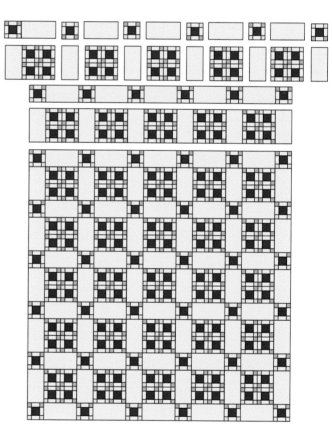

Block and Row Assembly

Finish the quilt

Refer to General Instructions, *pages 9—15,* to layer, baste, quilt, and bind the quilt.

Sweet Basil Finished Quilt Assembly

Finished size 54×72"

Select the fabric

3 yards light print

1-3/8 yards gold

1/2 yard dark red

1/2 yard light red

1/2 yard dark blue

1/4 yard green

3/4 yard binding

3-1/2 yards backing

Cut the fabric

1. From light print, cut
   4—8-1/2" strips; sew the strips end to end for a continuous length. From the length, cut
   3—44-1/2" lengths.

   7—3-1/2" strips; sew the strips end to end for a continuous length. From the length, cut
   6—44-1/2" lengths.

   8—2-1/2" strips. Sew 4 of the strips end to end for a continuous length. From the length, cut
   2—66-1/2" lengths for inner borders.

   14—1-1/2" strips.

2. From gold, cut
   27—1-1/2" strips.

3. From dark red, cut
   2—1-1/2" strips.

4. From light red, cut
   8—1-1/2" strips.

5. From dark blue, cut
   8—1-1/2" strips.

6. From green, cut
   4—1-1/2" strips.

Make 21 strip sets

1. Sew a gold 1-1/2" strip to each side of a light print 1-1/2" strip for 10 strip sets. Press seams toward the gold fabric. From the strip sets, cut 106—2-1/2" Unit A segments and 84—1-1/2" Unit B segments.

2. Sew a light red 1-1/2" strip to each long side of a gold 1-1/2" strip to make 4 strip sets. Press seams toward the gold fabric. From the strip sets, cut 54—2-1/2" Unit C segments.

3. Sew a dark red 1-1/2" strip to each long side of a gold 1-1/2" strip to make 1 strip set. Press seams toward the gold fabric. From the strip set, cut 28—1-1/2" Unit D segments.

4. Sew a dark blue 1-1/2" strip to each side of a gold 1-1/2" strip for 4 strip sets. Press seams toward the gold fabric. From the strip sets, cut 52—2-1/2" Unit E segments.

5. Sew a green 1-1/2" strip to each side of a gold 1-1/2" strip for 2 strip sets. Press seams toward the gold fabric. From the strip sets, cut 56—1-1/2" Unit F segments.

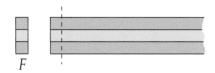

F

Assemble 26 of Block A and 26 of Block B

1. To make 26 of Block A, sew together units in this order: A, C, B, D, B, C, A.

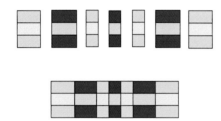

2. To make 26 of Block B, sew together units in this order: E, A, F, B, F, A, E.

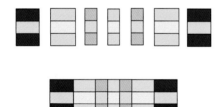

Assemble rows and borders

1. Alternating Block A and Block B, sew together 10 rows of 4 blocks each. Press seams in one direction.

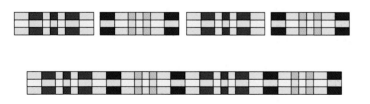

2. Join the rows alternately with 6—3-1/2×44-1/2" light print strips and 3—8-1/2×44-1/2" light print strips. Press seams in one direction.

3. Sew a Unit A and a Unit C to opposite ends of 2—66-1/2" light print lengths. Sew inner border lengths to each long side of the quilt. Press seams toward the inner border.

4. Make 2 each 4 Nine-Patch blocks, right sides together. Sew a Unit B to each side of a D unit, right sides together. Sew a Unit F to each side of a B unit. Press.

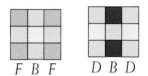

F B F   D B D

5. Alternating Block A and Block B, sew together 2 outer side borders. Sew alternate Nine-Patch blocks to the ends of each border. Sew borders to the sides of quilt. Press.

Finish the quilt

Refer to General Instructions, *pages 9–15,* to layer, baste, quilt, and bind the quilt.

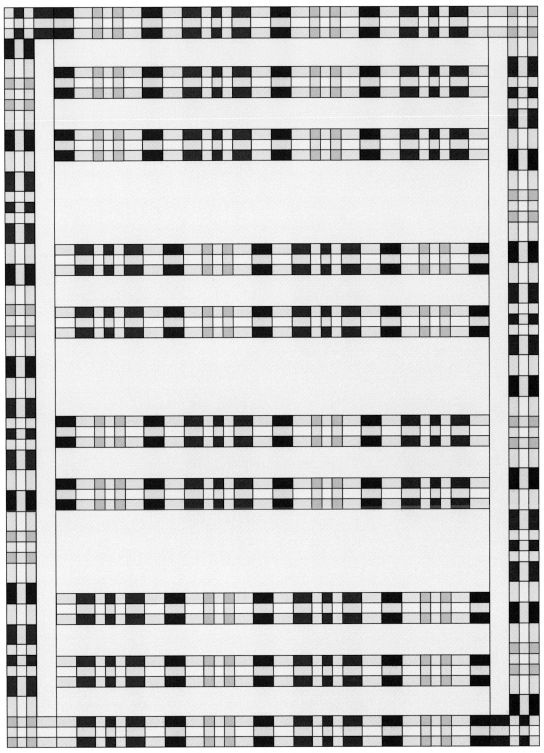

Thyme Finished Quilt Assembly

Thyme Quilting Designs

Thyme Quilting Design

Chicago Star

Ablaze with color to brighten winter decor, the magnificent design sparkles with holiday spirit. Quick cutting and piecing is a brilliant stroke to making these stars.

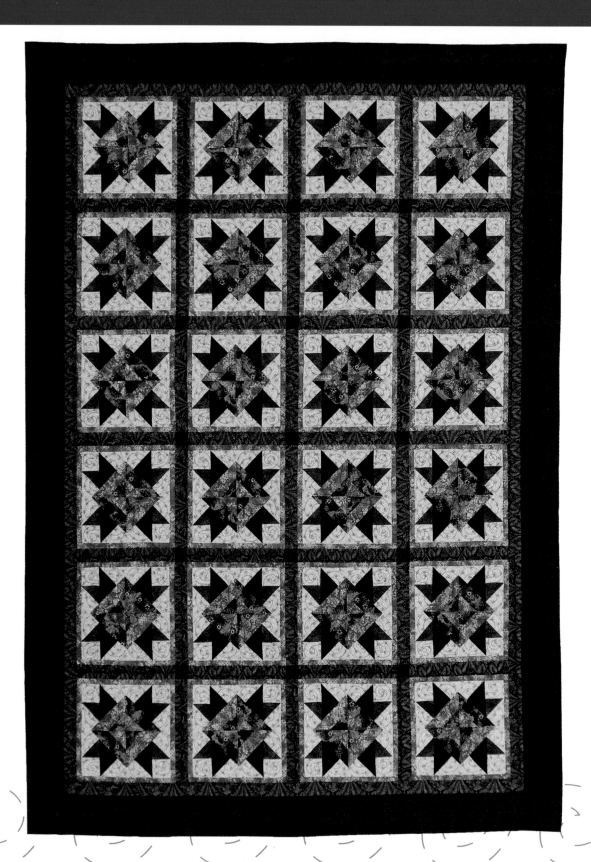

Finished size 54-1/4×76-1/4"
24—8-3/4" finished blocks

Select the fabric and supplies

2-1/2 yards red print for blocks, corner stones, outer border, and binding

1-2/3 yards ivory print for background

1-5/8 yards gold print

1/2 yard green print

1 yard green and red floral or leaf print

1-1/4 yards gold and black print

3-1/2 yards for backing

Companion Angle™

Cut the fabric

1. From red print, cut
   6—5" strips; sew the strips end to end for a continuous outer border length.

   7—2-1/2" strips; sew the strips end to end for a continuous binding length.

   3—4-3/4" strips; from the strips, cut 24—4-3/4" squares.

   1—1-3/4" strip; from the strip, cut 15—1-3/4" corner stone squares.

2. From ivory print, cut
   6—4-3/4" strips; from the strips, cut 48—4-3/4" squares. Set aside 24 squares. Cut the remaining 24 squares diagonally in quarters (in an X) for 96 triangles.

   5—3-3/4" strips; from the strips, cut 48—3-3/4" squares. Set aside 24 squares. Cut the remaining 24 squares diagonally in quarters (in an X) for 96 triangles.

3. From gold print, cut
   24—1" strips; from the strips, cut 48—9-1/4" lengths for block sides, and 48—10-1/4" lengths for block top and bottom.

   10—1-3/4" strips for spool blocks.

4. From green and red print, cut
   10—1-3/4" strips for spool blocks.

5. From green print, cut
   3—3-3/4" strips; from the strips, cut 24—3-3/4" squares.

6. From gold and black print, cut
   16—1-3/4" strips. From 10 of the strips, cut
   38—10-1/4" block sashing lengths. Sew the remaining 6 strips end to end for a continuous length.

Piece 24 Chicago Star blocks

1. Sew each gold print 1-3/4" strip to each green and red print 1-3/4" strip. Press seams toward the darker fabric. Use the Companion Angle™ and a rotary cutter to cut 48 gold base angles and 48 green/red base angles.

2. Sew the angles together in a square, half at a time, alternating color placement. Carefully press the seams in one direction to avoid distorting the square.

3. To make large half-square triangles, pair red 4-3/4" squares with ivory 4-3/4" squares. Draw an X on the wrong side of 12 red and 12 ivory squares. Sew 1/4" from the drawn lines. Cut apart on the drawn lines. Press seams toward the red fabric.

4. To make small half-square triangles, pair 24 green 3-3/4" squares with 24 ivory 3-3/4" squares. Draw an X on the wrong side of 12 green and 12 ivory squares. Refer to Step 3 *above* to make 96 green and ivory half-square triangles. Press seams toward the green fabric.

5. To make 48 Unit A triangle units, sew small half-square triangles to the right side of large half-square triangles. To make 48 Unit B triangles units, sew small half-square triangles to the left side of large half-square triangles. Press seams toward the darker fabric.

Unit A   Unit B

6. Sew a 4-3/4" ivory triangle to each side of the red-green-ivory Unit A and Unit B triangle units. Press seams toward the lighter fabric.

7. On each Unit A, measure 1-1/2" from the seam line on each side and cut off the extending triangle corners.

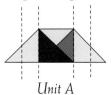

Unit A

8. Noting color placement, sew each Unit A to opposite sides of the center square from Step 2. Press seams toward the center square. Sew each Unit B to remaining sides of the block. Press seams toward the center square.

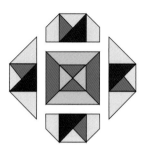

9. Sew a small ivory triangle to each block corner. Press seams toward the block corner.

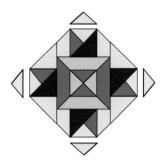

10. Sew a gold 9-1/4" strip to opposite sides of each block. Press. Sew a 10-1/4" length to the top and bottom of each block. Press.

Assemble rows, sashing, and borders

1. Lay out the blocks in 6 rows of 4 blocks each. Sew a 10-1/4" gold and black print sashing strip to join the blocks in each horizontal row. Press seams toward the sashing strips.

2. Sew together 5 rows of 4—10-1/4" gold and black print sashing strips with 3—1-3/4" red corner stone squares. Press.

3. Sew a long sashing strip between each row to join the rows. Press the quilt top without distorting the seams.

4. Measure the quilt top lengthwise through the center to determine inner border side lengths. From the continuous 1-3/4" gold and black print strip, cut 2 lengths to fit. Sew the lengths to each long side; press.

5. Measure the quilt top width through the center to determine top and bottom inner border lengths. Cut 2 lengths to fit and sew to the top and bottom of the quilt top. Press.

6. Measure the quilt top for 5" red outer borders, following Steps 4 and 5 to cut and sew the sides, then the top and bottom. Press seams to border.

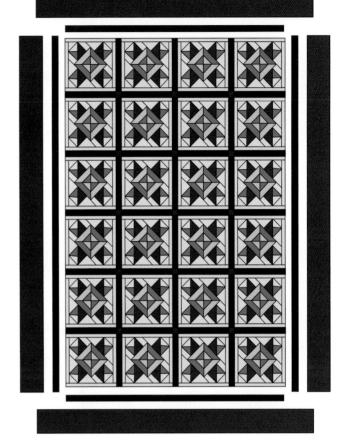

Row, Sashing, and Border Assembly

Finish the quilt

Refer to General Instructions, *pages 9–15*, to layer, baste, quilt, and bind the quilt.

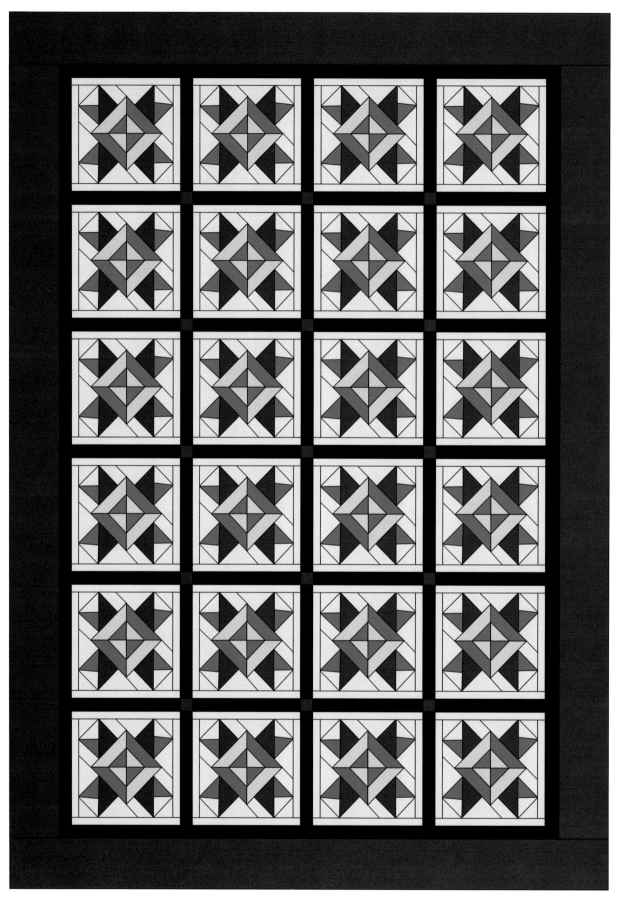

Chicago Star Finished Quilt Assembly

Chicago Star Quilting Design

Chilly Fellow

*In anticipation of building a snowy friend outdoors, stay warm and cozy indoors
to piece and dress a cuddly snow person—who will hold his shape in the sun.*

Finished size 35×62"

Select fabric and supplies

1-1/4 yards cream on white

1 yard dark blue

1-1/4 yards red for hat, scarf, inner border, and binding

5/8 yard blue plaid

1/3 yard brown plaid

1/8 yard gold

gray for mitten band

orange for carrot nose

Buttons: 3 @ 1-1/2", 2 @ 1", 5 @ 1/2"

Cut the fabric

1. From cream on white, cut
   1—15-1/2×23-1/2" rectangle
   1—11-1/2×14-1/2" rectangle
   1—5-1/2×11-1/2" rectangle
   2—6-1/2×7-1/2" rectangles
   1—3-1/2×9-1/2" rectangle
   2—1-1/2×9-1/2" rectangles
   1—2-1/2×6-1/2" rectangle
   1—2-1/2×13-1/2" rectangle
   2—1-1/2" squares.

2. From dark blue, cut:
   2—3-1/2" strips; from the strip, cut
      1—25-1/2" rectangle
      9—3-1/2" squares
      1—4-1/2" rectangle.

   3—2-1/2" strips; from the strips, cut
      2—25-1/2" rectangles
      2—10-1/2" rectangles

   2—6-1/2" rectangles
   2—4-1/2" rectangles
   2—2-1/2" squares
   4—1-1/2" rectangles.

   4—1-1/2" strips; from the strips, cut
      22—1-1/2" squares
      9—1-1/2×2-1/2" rectangles
      2—26-1/2" rectangles
      4—1-1/2×3-1/2" rectangles.

3. From red, cut
   5—2-1/2" strips; sew the strips end to end for a continuous binding length.

   5—1-1/2" strips; sew the strips end to end for a continuous inner border length.

   1—2-1/2" strip; from the strip, cut
      2—9-1/2" rectangles,
      2—1-1/2" rectangles, and
      1—6-1/2" rectangle.

   1—3-1/2×11-1/2" rectangle.
   1—4-1/2×11-1/2" rectangle.

4. From blue plaid, cut
   5—4-1/4" strips; sew the strips end to end for a continuous outer border length.

5. From brown plaid, cut
   1—2-1/2×11-1/2" rectangle.
   2—4-1/2×5-1/2" rectangles.
   2—1-1/2×3-1/2" rectangles.
   2—1-1/2×2-1/2" rectangles.

6. From gold, cut
   1—1-1/2" strip; from the strip, cut
      3—4-1/2" rectangles,
      3—2-1/2" rectangles, and
      6—1-1/2" squares.

7. From gray, cut
   2—1-1/2×4-1/2" rectangles.

Assemble Chilly Fellow

Section 1—Head

Note: Use template-free angle piecing (see General Instructions, page 13) to assemble Rows 1, 3, 4, 6, and 7.

Row 1. Sew dark blue 2-1/2×10-1/2" rectangles to each side of a red 2-1/2×9-1/2" hat rectangle.

Row 2. For the hat top, sew dark blue 1-1/2×2-1/2" rectangles to each side of a red 2-1/2×9-1/2" rectangle.

Row 3. For hat brim, sew dark blue 1-1/2" squares to each side of a brown plaid 2-1/2×11-1/2" rectangle.

Row 4. Sew brown plaid 1-1/2×2-1/2" rectangles to each end of a cream 1-1/2 x 9-1/2" rectangle. Trim and press. Sew dark blue 1-1/2" squares to each end.

Row 5. Sew dark blue 1-1/2×3-1/2" rectangles to each side of a cream 3-1/2×9-1/2" rectangle.

Row 6. Sew red 1-1/2×2-1/2" rectangles to each side of a cream 1-1/2×9-1/2" rectangle. Press. Sew dark blue 1-1/2" squares to each side.

Row 7. Sew cream 1-1/2" squares to each side of a red 3-1/2×11-1/2" scarf rectangle.

Join Rows 2 through 7 only.

Section 2—Arms

Note: Use template-free angle piecing for Units A, B, and C.

Unit A. Sew dark blue 1-1/2" squares to brown plaid 4-1/2×5-1/2" rectangles for mittens. Sew gray 1-1/2×4-1/2" rectangles to the lower edge of each mitten.

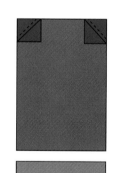

Unit B. Sew dark blue 1-1/2×3-1/2" rectangles to brown plaid 1-1/2×3-1/2" rectangles, mirror image. Sew dark blue 1-1/2×2-1/2" rectangles to opposite ends of the brown plaid for mitten thumbs.

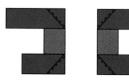

Unit C. Sew dark blue 3-1/2" squares to two cream 6-1/2×7-1/2" rectangles, mirror image. Sew dark blue 2-1/2" squares to opposite corners of the cream rectangles, mirror image.

Refer to the diagram, *below,* to lay out right and left arms. Sew on the dark blue 2-1/2×6-1/2" rectangles.

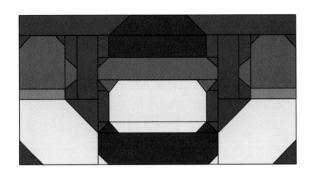

Sew a Section 2 to each side of Section 1. Sew Row 1 to the top of the joined sections.

Section 3—Scarf and Lower Body

Note: Use template-free angle piecing for all rows.

Row 1. Sew a dark blue 2-1/2×4-1/2" rectangle to a cream 2-1/2×13-1/2" rectangle.

Sew a red 2-1/2×6-1/2" rectangle to the opposite end.

Sew a cream 2-1/2×6-1/2" rectangle to the red end. Sew a dark blue 2-1/2×4-1/2" rectangle to the cream.

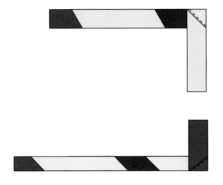

Row 2. Sew a dark blue 3-1/2" square to a cream 11-1/2×14-1/2" rectangle. Sew a dark blue 3-1/2" square to a cream 5-1/2×11-1/2" rectangle. Sew a unit to each side of a red 4-1/2×11-1/2" scarf rectangle.

Row 3. Sew dark blue 3-1/2" squares to cream 15-1/2×23-1/2" rectangle. Sew Row 2 to Row 3.

To complete Section 3, sew dark blue 1-1/2×26-1/2" rectangles to each side. Sew Row 1 to the top of the section. Sew a dark blue 2-1/2×25-1/2" rectangle to the bottom.

Section 4—Stars

Note: Use template-free angle piecing for all rows.

Row 1. Sew dark blue 1-1/2×2-1/2" rectangles to each side of 3 gold 1-1/2×2-1/2" rectangles.

Row 2. Sew dark blue 1-1/2" squares to each side of 3 gold 1-1/2×4-1/2" rectangles.

Row 3. Sew gold 1-1/2" squares to each side of 3 dark blue 1-1/2×2-1/2" rectangles. Sew a dark blue 1-1/2" square to each side. Join the rows together to make 3 stars.

Sew dark blue 3-1/2" squares between star blocks and at one end of the row. Sew a dark blue 3-1/2×4-1/2" rectangle to the opposite long end of the row. Press. Sew a dark blue 3-1/2×25-1/2" rectangle to the bottom of the star row.

Sew a dark blue 2-1/2×25-1/2" rectangle to the top of the star row.

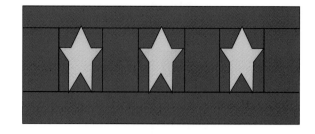

Sew Section 4 to the top of the quilt. Sew Section 3 to the bottom of the quilt. Press.

Sew on the Borders

1. Measure lengthwise through the center to determine side inner border lengths. Cut 2 red strips to fit; sew one to each side; press toward the border. Measure widthwise for top and bottom inner border lengths. Cut 2 red strips to fit; sew to the top and bottom; press toward the border.

2. Measure, cut, and sew blue plaid outer borders to the sides, then to the top and bottom of the quilt top, as for the inner border.

Finish the quilt

1. Cut and appliqué carrot nose. Sew on button for eyes, mouth, and down the front. Embroider star lines. Cut or tear 1/2×7" strips for scarf fringe; knot strips and sew to scarf end.

2. Refer to General Instructions, *pages 9–15*, to layer, baste, quilt, and bind the quilt.

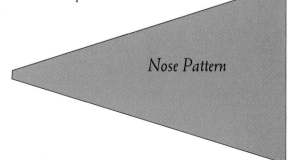

Nose Pattern

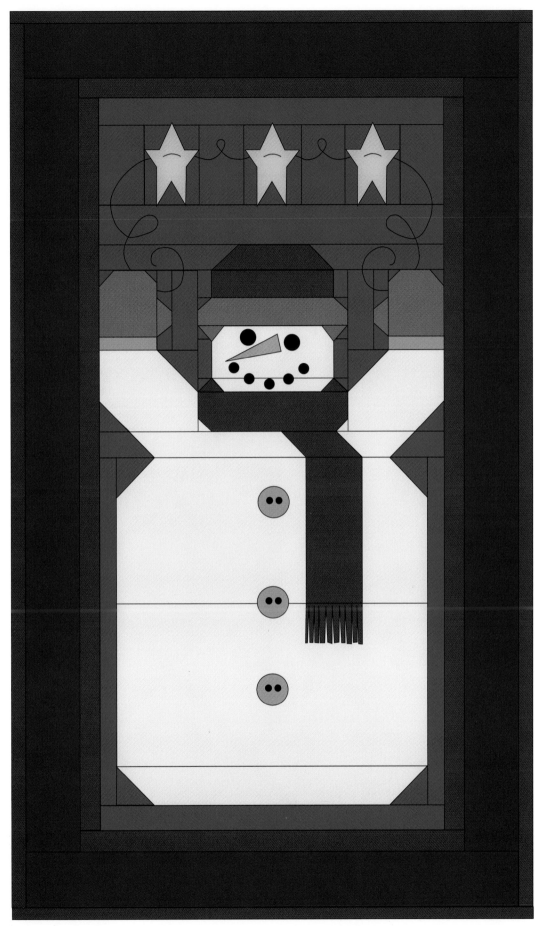

Chilly Fellow Finished Quilt Assembly

Freezin' Season Snowmen

Versatile Log Cabin blocks are a warm home for appliquéd little snow folks and companion snowflakes. For personality, dress each snow person individually in his own plaid vest.

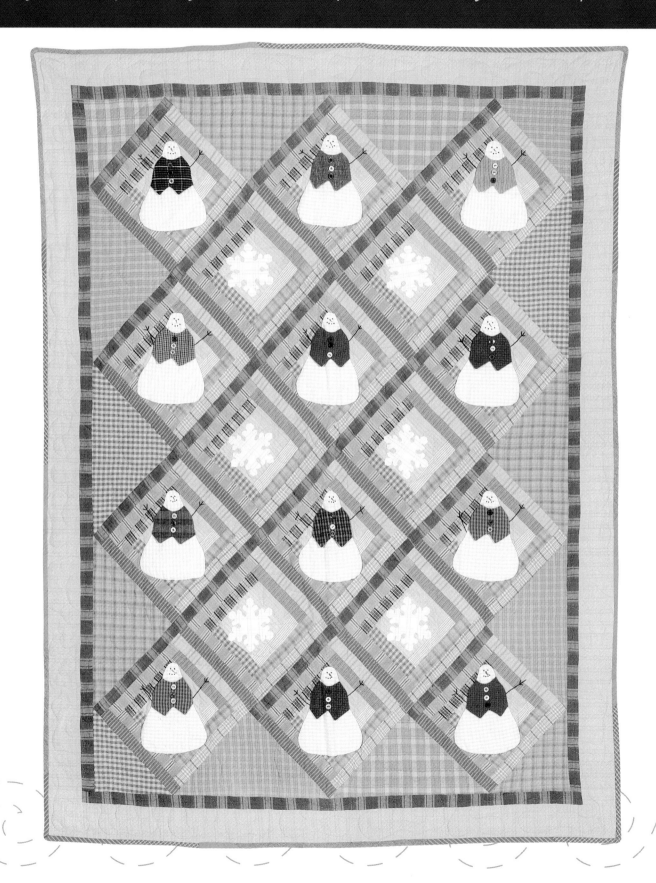

Finished size 59× 77"

Select fabric and notions

This quilt is made from assorted plaid flannels.

1-1/2 yards cream on white

1/2 yard light plaid (for block centers)

1/4 yard each of 6 light plaids

2/3 yard each of 4 medium plaids

1/4 yard each of 2 medium plaids

1/4 yard of assorted contrasting
plaids for snowmen vests

3/8 yard rust plaid for inner border

3/4 yard pale gold for outer border

5/8 yard taupe plaid for binding

3-1/2 yards for backing

Buttons—36 assorted sizes, shapes, and colors

Embroidery floss—black, orange, and off-white

Fusible webbing material

Cut the fabric

1. From medium plaids, cut
    3—15-1/2" squares; cut each square
    diagonally twice (in an X) to make
    12 setting triangles (10 will be used).

    2—8" squares; cut each square
    diagonally once to make 4 corner
    triangles.

2. From light plaids, cut
    2—4-1/2" strips; from the strips, cut
    18—4-1/2" center squares.

23—1-1/2" strips. From the strips, cut
and sort 18 each of the following sizes
by length and block position:

#2—4-1/2" rectangles
#3—5-1/2" rectangles
#6—6-1/2" rectangles
#7—7-1/2" rectangles
#10—8-1/2" rectangles
#11—9-1/2" rectangles

3. From medium plaids, cut
    23—1-1/2" strips. From the strips, cut
    and sort 18 each of the following sizes
    by length and block position:

    #4—5-1/2" rectangles
    #5—6-1/2" rectangles
    #8—7-1/2" rectangles
    #9—8-1/2" rectangles
    #12—9-1/2" rectangles
    #13—10-1/2" rectangles

4. From rust plaid, cut
    7—1-1/2" strips; sew the strips end to
    end for a continuous length.

5. From pale gold, cut
    7—3" strips; sew the strips end to end
    for a continuous length.

6. From taupe plaid, cut
    8—2-1/2" strips; sew the strips end to
    end for a continuous binding length.

7. Trace and cut out the snowmen
    pattern, *page 196*, to template material.
    Fold the cream on white flannel fabric
    in half, right sides together. Trace and
    cut out 12 snowmen (doubled).

    Trace and cut out the snowflake
    pattern on template material. Trace
    6 snowflakes onto fusible webbing.
    Place the webbing on the wrong side
    of the cream on white flannel and cut
    out 6 snowflakes.

8. Trace the snowmen vest pattern to
    template material. Cut out the pattern.

Fold assorted plaids in half, right sides together, and cut out 12 coubled vests.

Sew 18 Log Cabin Blocks

1. Sew the light plaid and medium plaid strips to each light 4-1/2" center square in ascending order of length, sewing strips clockwise around the center square beginning with light strips. For quick piecing, use the chain-piecing method (see Basic Instructions). Press, and proceed to the next lengths. After the #5 Log Cabin strip is sewn to the block, the block should measure 6-1/2" square.

   Sew Log Cabin strips #6 to #9 to the block. The block should measure 8-1/2" square.

   Sew Log Cabin strips #10 to #13 to the block. The block should measure 10-1/2" square. Press the blocks without distorting the seams and raw edges. Set the blocks aside.

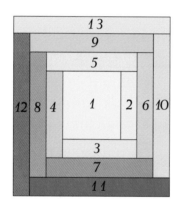

Sew Snowmen and vests

1. Right sides together, sew around the upper and lower edges of the vest, leaving both sides open. Turn the vest to the right side and press, rolling the seams to the underside.

2. Separate the snowmen. Right sides up, pin each vest to a single snowman layer. Cut a vertical slit in the remaining single snowman layers; match them to snowmen with vests, right sides together. Pin around the edges. Sew 1/8" from the edge, catching vest sides in the seams. Clip curves close to the seam without cutting through the seam, and turn each snowman to the right side through the slit. Press, rolling the seam toward the underside.

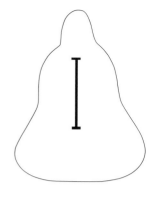

3. Embroider faces on the right side of each snowman.

Appliqué Snowmen and Snowflakes to Log Cabin blocks

1. Hand appliqué the 12 snowmen to Log Cabin blocks, noting block light and medium color placement. Use black embroidery floss to backstitch Snowmen arms.

2. Fuse the 6 snowflakes to Log Cabin blocks. Appliqué close to the edges around each snowflake.

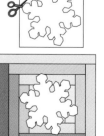

Assemble the rows

1. For Row 1 and Row 6, sew 2 setting triangles then 1 corner triangle to each of 2 Snowman Log Cabin blocks, noting light and medium strip placement. Press seams toward the triangles.

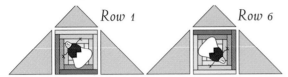

2. Sew together 2 rows of 3 Log Cabin blocks each, with a snowflake block between snowmen blocks, noting light and medium strip placement. Press the seams flat. To complete Row 2 and Row 5, sew a setting triangle to the ends of each row, noting the triangle direction for each row.

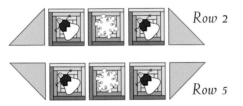

3. Sew together 2 rows of 5 Log Cabin blocks each, beginning and ending each row with snowmen blocks with alternate snowflake blocks between, noting light and medium strip placement. Press the seams flat. To complete Row 3 and Row 4, sew a setting triangle to one end of each row and a corner triangle to the opposite end of each row.

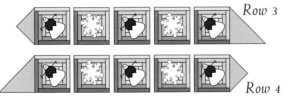

4. Sew the diagonal rows together. Press the seams without distorting the bias seams.

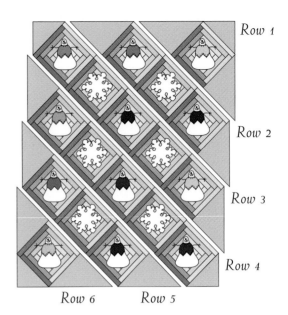

5. Measure 1/4" from the seam points and trim along the edges of the quilt top, using a rotary ruler and cutter or a yardstick and scissors. Baste 1/8" along the edge of the quilt top to stabilize.

Sew on the borders

1. Measure the length of the quilt top through the center for side border lengths. Cut 2 inner border strips to fit; sew one to each side. Press seams toward the borders.

2. Measure the width of the quilt top through the center for top and bottom border lengths. Cut 2 strips to fit; sew to the top and bottom. Press seams toward the borders.

3. Measure, cut, and sew outer borders first to the sides, then to the top and bottom of the quilt top as for the inner borders. Press seams toward the inner borders.

Finish the quilt

Refer to General Instructions, *pages 9–15*, to layer, baste, quilt, and bind the quilt.

Sew the buttons on the snowmen through all layers of the quilt.

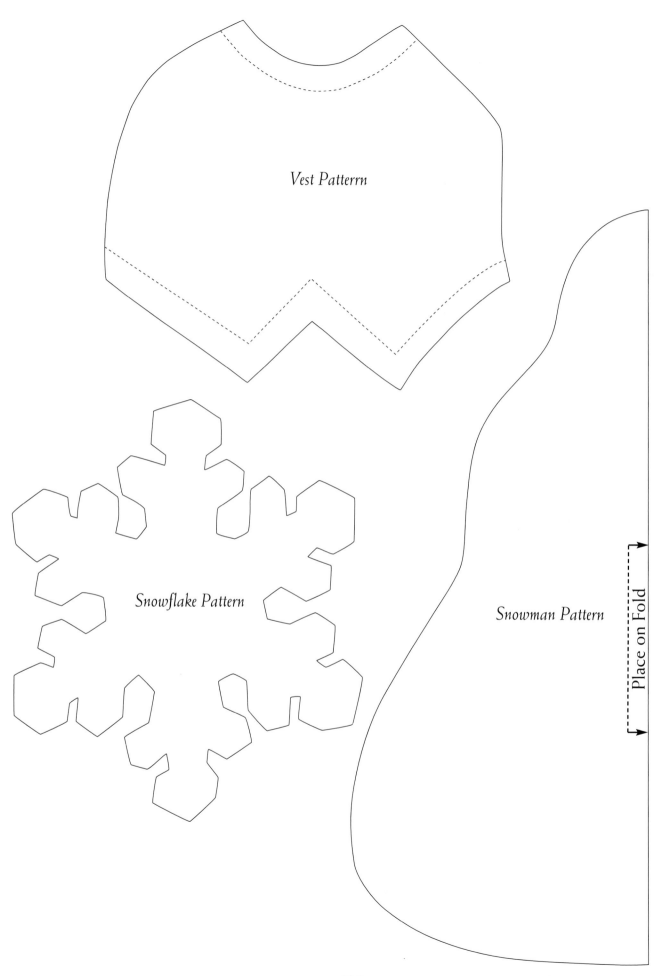

Vest Pattern

Snowflake Pattern

Snowman Pattern

Place on Fold

Freezin' Season Snowmen Finished Quilt Assembly

Southern Spice

Cook up a holiday favorite that contains no calories. This sugar-and-spice and all-
things-nice interpretation will nourish your creative quilting appetite.

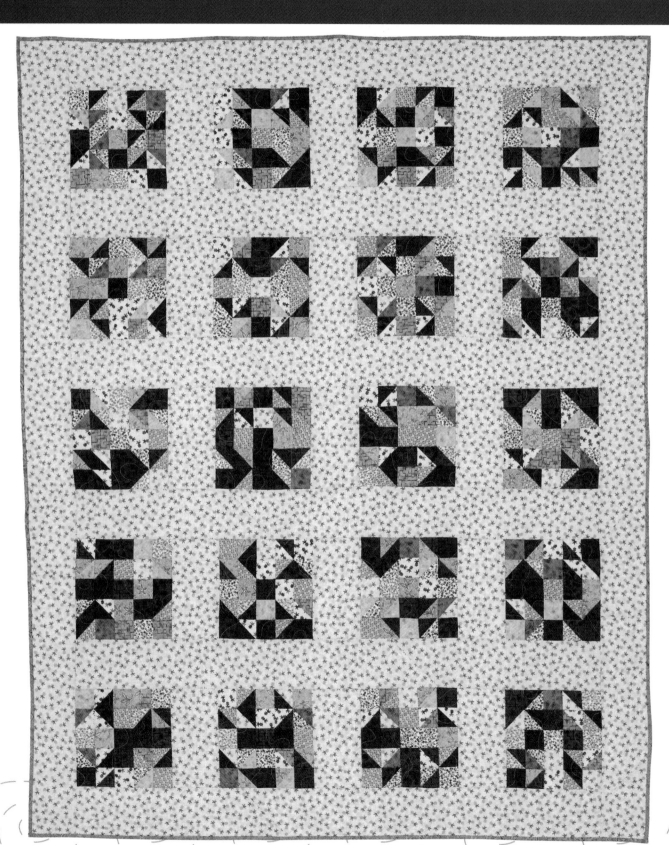

Finished size 65×80"

Select the fabric

10 assorted light fat quarters (18×22")

10 assorted dark fat quarters (18×22")

*3-1/4 yards light print background
for sashing and borders*

2/3 yard green for binding

4 yards for backing

Cut the fabric

1. From each light fat quarter, cut
   2—2-1/2" strips
   4—2-1/2" squares
   6—3×6" rectangles

2. From each dark fat quarter, cut
   2—2-1/2" strips
   4—2-1/2" squares
   6—3×6" rectangles

3. From light print background, cut
   19—5-1/2" strips. From 4 of the strips,
   cut 15—10-1/2" rectangles. Sew the
   remaining strips end to end for a
   continuous length.

4. From green, cut
   8—2-1/2" strips. Sew the strips end to
   end for a continuous binding length.

Make 240 half-square triangles

1. Right sides together, align each light
   3×6" rectangle with each dark 3×6"
   rectangle. On the wrong side of the

light fabric, draw a vertical line to
mark 2—3" squares. Draw diagonal
lines from one end of the center line
to opposite corners. Stitch 1/4" from
each side of the diagonal lines.

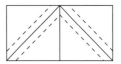

2. Cut along the marked lines. Remove
   stitching along triangle points. Press
   seams to set, then open triangles and
   press seam toward the dark fabric.
   Trim triangle squares to 2-1/2".

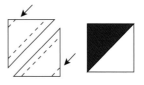

Make 8 strip sets

1. Sew together 3 strip sets, using
   5 assorted light and dark 2-1/2" strips
   for each strip set. Press seams in one
   direction. From the strip sets, cut
   20—2-1/2" segments.

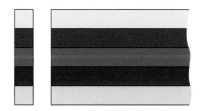

2. Sew together 5 strip sets, using
   2 assorted light and/or dark 2-1/2"
   strips for each strip sets. Press seams
   toward the lighter fabric. From the
   strip sets, cut 40—2-1/2" segments.

Sew 20 Southern Spice blocks

1. Mixing color arrangements of triangle squares and 2-1/2" squares, assemble 20 each of Unit A, B, C, and D, noting position of triangles within squares.

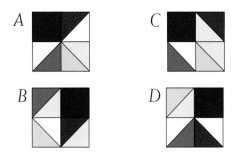

2. Using Units A and B, 1 long strip set, and 2 short strip sets, sew together Block 1.

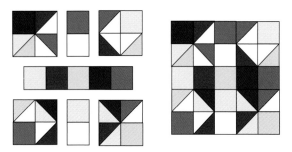

3. Using Units C and D, 1 long strip set, and 2 short strip sets, sew together Block 2.

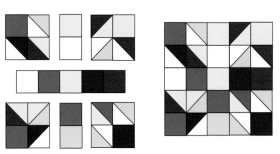

Join the blocks with sashing and borders

1. Lay out 5 rows of 4 blocks each with short sashing strips. Sew each row of blocks to the short sashing strips between the block. Press seams toward the sashing.

2. Cut 2—5-1/2" sashing strips 55" long. Sew sashing strips to join the rows. Press seams toward the sashing.

3. Measure the length of the quilt top through the center to determine side border lengths; cut borders to fit. Sew a border to each side of the quilt; press seams toward the borders.

4. Measure the width of the quit top through the center to determine top and bottom border lengths; cut borders to fit. Sew a border to the top and to the bottom; press seams toward the borders.

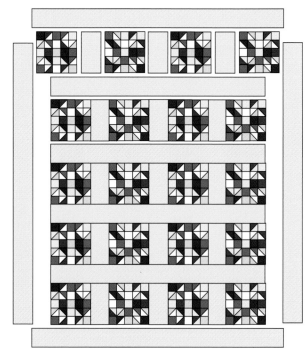

Block and Row Assembly

Finish the quilt

Refer to General Instructions, *pages 9–15*, to layer, baste, quilt, and bind the quilt.

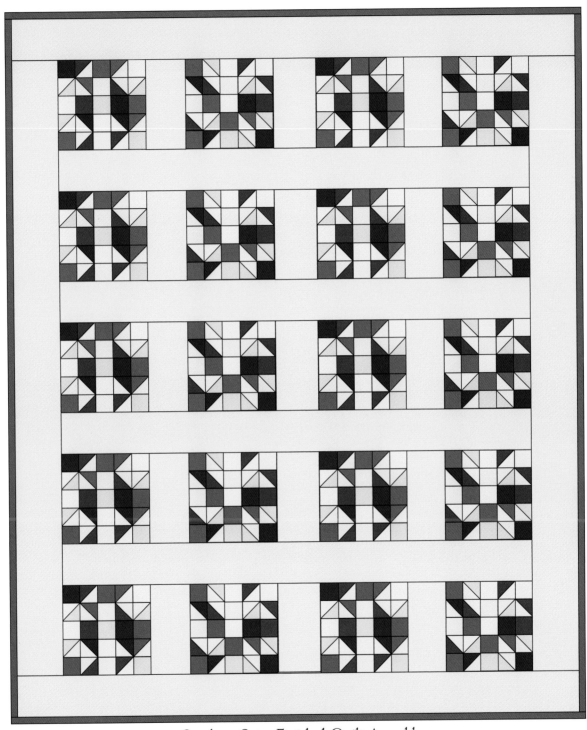

Southern Spice Finished Quilt Assembly

Twilight

Dream of golden summer evenings nestled under this cozy quilt full of traditional blocks: Flying Geese, Bear's Paw, Friendship Star, Ohio Star, and Log Cabin.

Finished size 60" square

Select the fabric

3/4 yard gold print

4-1/2 yards total of assorted light, medium, and dark prints

1-1/4 yards of tan

1-1/4 yards of gray/dark tan

1 yard black with tiny stars or print

3-3/4 yards for backing

Cut the fabric for 8 Sunshine Star Blocks

Note: Label and stack fabric colors and sizes.

1. From gold print, cut 3—2" strips; from the strips, cut 64—2" B squares.

   1—4-3/4" strip; from the strip, cut 8—4-3/4" A squares.

   2—2-3/8" strips; from the strips, cut 32—2-3/8" squares. Cut each square in half diagonally for 64 triangles.

   1—4-1/4" strip; from the strip, cut 8—4-1/4" squares. Cut each square diagonally twice (in an X) for 32 D triangles.

2. From assorted dark prints, cut 4—2-3/8" strips; from the strips, cut 64—2-3/8" squares. Cut each square in half diagonally for 128 C triangles.

3. From assorted medium prints, cut 2—2-3/8" strips; from the strips, cut 32—2-3/8" squares. Cut each square in half diagonally for 64 C triangles.

Sew Sunshine Star blocks

1. Sew 2 C triangles to adjacent sides of 32—2" squares to make 32 corner units. Use 4 units for each block.

2. Sew a corner unit to each side of 8—4-3/4" gold squares.

3. Sew together 1 gold and 1 medium C triangle to make 8 half-square triangles for each block (64 triangle squares total). Press seams toward dark fabric.

4. Sew 2 dark C triangles to each side of a gold D triangle to make a Flying Geese unit. Press the seams toward the large triangle. The pieced unit should measure 2×3-1/2". Make 4 Flying Geese units for each block (32 Flying Geese units total).

5. Lay out the center units, the triangle squares, the Flying Geese units, and 4—2" gold squares for each block. Sew the units together in side, top, and bottom sections.

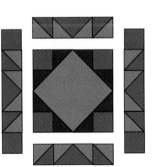

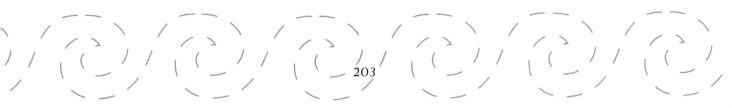

Sew the sections to the center unit. Press seams toward the outer edges. Each Sunshine Block should measure 9-1/2" square.

Cut the fabric and make a Friendship Star block

Note: Use two contrasting colors for each block. Follow the instructions below to make 1 block.

1. From fabric for star background, cut
   4—2" squares
   2—2×3-1/2" rectangles.

2. From fabric for the star, cut
   2—2" squares
   1—2×5" rectangle

3. Place fine-grit sandpaper beneath the fabric (to prevent fabric from slipping or stretching) and mark a diagonal line on the wrong side of 2—2" background squares and both 2" star fabric squares.

4. Right sides together, align a 2" star fabric square along one side of a 2×3-1/2" background rectangle, noting diagonal line direction. Stitch on the line, trim seam allowance to 1/4", press the seam to set it, then press the triangle open to make a Unit A rectangle. Repeat to make a second Unit A rectangle. Sew a 2" square to star end of each unit.

5. Right sides together, align a 2" background square along each end of the 2×5" star fabric rectangle, noting diagonal line direction. Stitch on the lines, trim seam allowances to 1/4", press the seam to set it, then press the triangle open to make a Unit B rectangle.

6. Lay out the 2 Unit A rectangles and the Unit B rectangle. Sew the units together to complete 1—5" square Friendship Star Block.

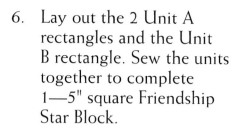

7. Repeat the instructions above to complete 25—5"-square Friendship Star Blocks.

Cut the fabric and make a Bear's Paw block

Note: Use two contrasting colors for each block. Follow the instructions below to make 1 block.

1. From background fabric, cut
   2—2-3/8" squares; cut each square in half diagonally for 4 triangles.

   1—2" square.

2. From fabric for paws, cut
   2—2-3/8" squares; cut each square in half diagonally for 4 triangles.

   1—3-1/2" square.

3. Sew together each background fabric triangle and each paw triangle to make 4 triangle-squares. The units should measure 2" square.

4. Lay out the units with the background and paw squares. Sew the block together in sections. The pieced Bear's Paw block should measure 5" square.

5. Repeat above instructions to complete 25—5"-square Bear's Paw blocks.

Cut the fabric and make 2 Log Cabin blocks

1. From assorted prints, cut
   2—2-1/2×3" center rectangles, #1
   2—1-1/2×3" rectangles, #2
   2—1-1/2×3-1/2" rectangles, #3
   2—1-1/2×4" rectangles, #4
   2—1-1/2×4-1/2" rectangles, #5
   4—1-1/2×5" rectangles, #6 and #7.

2. Right sides together, sew rectangles in sequential order, pressing after each addition. The finished blocks should measure 5×5-1/2".

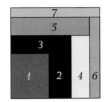

Cut the fabric and make an Ohio Star block

Note: Use 2 contrasting colors and a background tan to make each of the blocks. For the varied tan background shown in the quilt, make 10 blocks with tan and 10 with gray/dark tan. The following instructions are for cutting and making 1 block.

1. From tan, cut
   4—2" squares
   4—2 x 3-1/2" rectangles.

2. From fabric for star center, cut
   1—3-1/2" square.

3. From fabric for star points, cut
   8—2" squares

4. Lay the 8—2" squares for star points right side down on fine-grit sandpaper. Mark a diagonal line on the squares.

5. Right sides together, note diagonal line direction, and align a 2" square on a 2×3-1/2" tan rectangle. Sew on the line, press to set the seam, trim seam to 1/4", and press toward dark fabric.

6. Right sides together, align a second 2" marked square along the opposite end of the 2×3-1/2" tan rectangle. Sew along the line, press, trim the seam to 1/4", open the triangle, and press again to complete a 2×3-1/2" Flying Geese unit. Repeat to make 4 Flying Geese units for each Ohio Star Block.

7. Lay out the 3-1/2" center square, 4 Flying Geese units and 4—2" tan squares. Sew the units together to complete a 6-1/2" Ohio Star Block.

8. Repeat the instructions above to make 20—6-1/2"-Ohio Star Blocks.

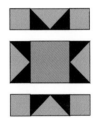

Assemble the quilt center

1. Sew together 4 Sunshine Star Blocks in two rows of two blocks, pressing seams in opposite directions. Join the rows; press. The center unit should measure 18-1/2" square.

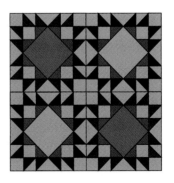

Cut and sew 5 borders around Sunshine Center

First Border

1. From assorted prints, cut 20—1-1/2" strips in 6" to 8" lengths.

   Sew the strips end to end for a continuous length. From the continuous length, cut 2—1-1/2×20-1/2" and 2—1-1/2×18-1/2" border strips.

2. Sew shorter strips to opposite sides of the center block. Press seams toward the strips. Sew longer strips to the top and bottom of the center block; press seams toward the strips.

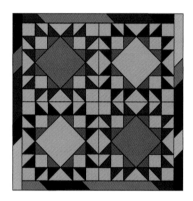

Second Border

1. From assorted prints, cut 12—2×2-1/2" rectangles.

2. Sew together 4 Friendship Star blocks and 3 assorted print 2×2-1/2" rectangles. Press seams in one direction. Sew the 5×20-1/2" border to the bottom of the quilt. Press the seam toward the first border.

3. Sew together 4 Bear's Paw blocks and 3 assorted print 2×2-1/2" rectangles.

Press seams in one direction. Sew the 5×20-1/2" border to the left side of the quilt. Press Press the seam toward the first border.

4. Sew together 6 Friendship Star blocks and 3 assorted print 2×2-1/2" rectangles. Press seams in one direction; sew the 5×29-1/2" border to the top of the quilt. Press the seam toward the first border.

5. Sew together 6 Bear's Paw blocks and three assorted print 2×2-1/2" rectangles. Press seams in one direction; sew the 5×29-1/2" border to the bottom of the quilt. Press the seam toward the first border.

Third Border

1. From black with tiny stars or print, cut 2—2×32-1/2" strips 2—2×29-1/2" strips.

2. Sew shorter strips to opposite sides of the quilt top. Press seams toward the black border.

3. Sew longer strips to the top and bottom of the quilt top; press seams toward the black border.

Fourth Border

1. From assorted prints, cut 2—1×5" rectangles.

2. Sew together 7 Bear's Paw blocks and 1—1×5" rectangle for a 5×32-1/2" long side border. Press seams in one direction; sew the border to the right side of the quilt top. Press seams toward the black border.

3. Sew together 7 Friendship Star blocks and 1—1×5" rectangle for a 5×32-1/2" long side border. Press seams in one direction; sew the border to the left side of the quilt top. Press seams toward the black border.

4. Sew together 8 Bear's Paw blocks and 1 Log Cabin block. Press seams in one direction and sew the 5×41-1/2" border to the top of the quilt. Press seams toward the black border.

5. Sew together 8 Friendship Star blocks and 1 Log Cabin block. Press seams in one direction; sew the 5×41-1/2" border to the bottom of the quilt. Press seams toward the black border.

Fifth Border

1. From tan, cut
   8—2×6-1/2" rectangles
   4—4-1/2×8" rectangles
   2—3-1/2×9-1/2" rectangles
   2—3-1/2×6-1/2" rectangles.

2. From gray/dark tan, cut
   8—2×6-1/2" rectangles
   4—4-1/2×8" rectangles
   2—3-1/2×9-1/2" rectangles
   2—3-1/2×6-1/2" rectangles.

3. From black with tiny stars or print, cut
   8—2×16-1/2" rectangles.

Sew the blocks together

1. Lay out 2—2×6-1/2" tan rectangles, 1—4-1/2×8" tan rectangle, 2 Ohio Star blocks with tan, and a black 2×16-1/2" rectangle. Sew the blocks and rectangles together.

2. Lay out 2—2×6-1/2" gray/dark tan rectangles, 1—4-1/2×8" gray/dark tan rectangle, 2 Ohio Star blocks with gray/dark tan, and a black 2×16-1/2" rectangle. Sew the blocks and rectangles together.

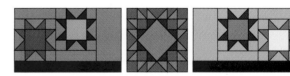

3. Sew the two pieced sections to opposite sides of a Sunshine Star block to make a 9-1/2×41-1/2" border unit. Repeat to make a second border unit. Sew the borders to the top and bottom of the quilt top. Press.

4. Lay out 2—2×6-1/2" tan rectangles, 1—3-1/2×6-1/2" tan rectangle, 1—3-1/2×9-1/2" tan rectangle, 1—4-1/2×8" tan rectangle, 3 Ohio Star blocks with tan, and a black 2×16-1/2" rectangle. Sew the blocks and rectangles together to measure 9-1/2×59-1/2".

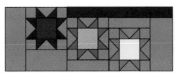 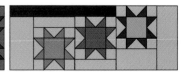

5. Sew the pieced borders to each side of the quilt. Press the seams toward the borders.

Finish the quilt

1. From black with stars or print, cut 6—2-1/2" strips; sew the strips end to end for a continuous binding length.

2. Refer to General Instructions, *pages 9–15*, to layer, baste, quilt, and bind the quilt.

Center and Border Assembly

Twilight Finished Quilt Assembly

Twilight Quilting Design

Twilight Quilting Design

Twilight Quilting Designs

Twilight Quilting Design

Butterfly

Welcome spring with printed pastels that seem to awaken and flutter across soft background fabric. Such natural elements enhance home decor year-round.

Finished size 58×76"
Finished blocks 8-3/4" square

Select the fabric

Use assorted pastel fabrics for a vintage look. The center block accent unifies the assortment and provides movement to the quilt.

30 assorted pastel print fat quarters (18×22")
or 1/4 yard of 30 assorted pastels prints
for blocks

1/8 yellow solid for center squares
and inner border

1-1/4 yards periwinkle for outer border

1-1/2 yards assorted pastel prints for
butterfly appliques and binding

4 yards backing fabric

1-1/2 yard lightweight fusible adhesive

Assorted pastel prints for butterflies

Embroidery floss or monofilament thread
to appliqué butterflies

Note: Although the block is easy to assemble, take time to plan the layout and match the inner edge of each block to the adjacent block. Use the Planning Diagram, page 218, to determine color placement, filling in sample blocks with fabric scraps or colored pencil to achieve the desired effect. Designate four colors—A, B, C, and D—to each block and note the color position as it relates to an adjacent block. Cut the required number of strip lengths for each block (see Diagram, page 216), and assemble the blocks in order of strip length from the center square outward, sewing same-size strips to opposite sides of the block. Press the seams toward the center block before sewing on additional strips.

Cut the fabric

1. From each pastel fat quarter, cut 10—1-1/4" strips (or cut 5—1-1/4" strips from each 1/4 yard cut).

2. From yellow solid, cut 2—1-3/4" strips; from the strips, cut 35—1-3/4" squares for block centers.

   6—1" strips; sew the strips end to end for a continuous length.

3. From periwinkle, cut 6—6" strips; sew the strips end to end for a continuous length.

4. From assorted pastel prints, cut 6—2-1/2" strips; sew the strips end to end for a continuous binding length.

Make 35 Stepping Stone blocks

1. Note color positions of the blocks and label fabric strips alphabetically and numerically to correspond to the Quilt Planning Diagram. From the pastel 1-1/4" strips, cut and sort lengths from 4 different colors.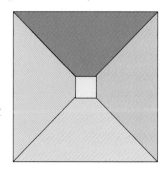

   From Fabric A and Fabric B, cut the following rectangles:
   1-3/4",
   3-1/4",
   4-3/4",
   6-1/4", and
   7-3/4".

From Fabric C and Fabric D, cut the following rectangles:
3-1/4",
4-3/4",
6-1/4",
7-3/4", and
9-1/4".

2. Sew a 1-3/4" Fabric A and a 1-3/4" Fabric B to opposite sides of a 1-3/4" yellow center square. Press seams toward the center.

3. Sew 3-1/4" Fabric C and D to each remaining side; press seams toward center. Sew strips in ascending length to blocks sides, noting color placement. Press at each step.

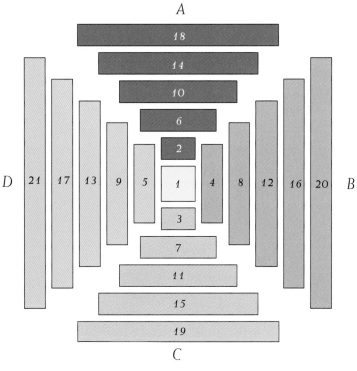

Assemble rows and border

1. Lay out the Stepping Stone blocks in 7 rows of 5 blocks, using the Planning Diagram, *page 218*, as a guide.

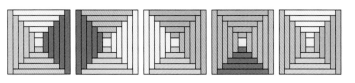

2. Sew each row of blocks, pressing seams in alternate directions from adjacent rows. Sew the rows together. Press the seams in one direction.

3. Measure the quilt lengthwise through the center; cut 2 yellow inner border lengths to fit each side. Sew to the quilt top; press seams toward the border. Measure the quilt widthwise through the center; cut 2 yellow inner border lengths to fit the top and bottom. Sew to the quilt top; press seams toward the border.

4. Measure the quilt lengthwise through the center; cut 2 periwinkle lengths to fit each side. Sew to the quilt top and press the seams toward the outer border. Measure the quilt widthwise through the center; cut 2 periwinkle lengths to fit the top and bottom; sew one to the top and one to the bottom. Press seams toward the outer border.

216

Appliqué the Butterflies

Note: To hand-appliqué the butterflies, cut templates 1/4" larger all around than the patterns.

1. Trace the Butterfly patterns, *page 220*, onto the paper side of fusible adhesive. Cut around the shapes approximately 1/8" beyond the designs.

2. Fuse adhesive to the wrong side of fabric. Cut out on the design lines. Remove paper backing. Position the butterflies on the quilt top, layering sections, and randomly overlapping borders. Press the butterfly fabrics to adhere the fusible webbing, using a press cloth and a dry iron.

3. Appliqué around the butterfly shapes by hand or machine, using coordinating threads, or machine appliqué using monofilament thread for the top thread and polyester thread in the bobbin.

Finish the quilt

Refer to General Instructions, *page 9–15*, to layer, baste, quilt, and bind the quilt top.

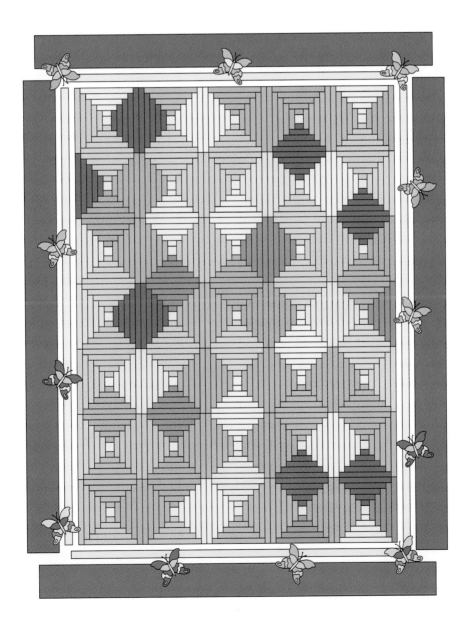

*Butterfly Quilt
Row and
Border
Assembly*

217

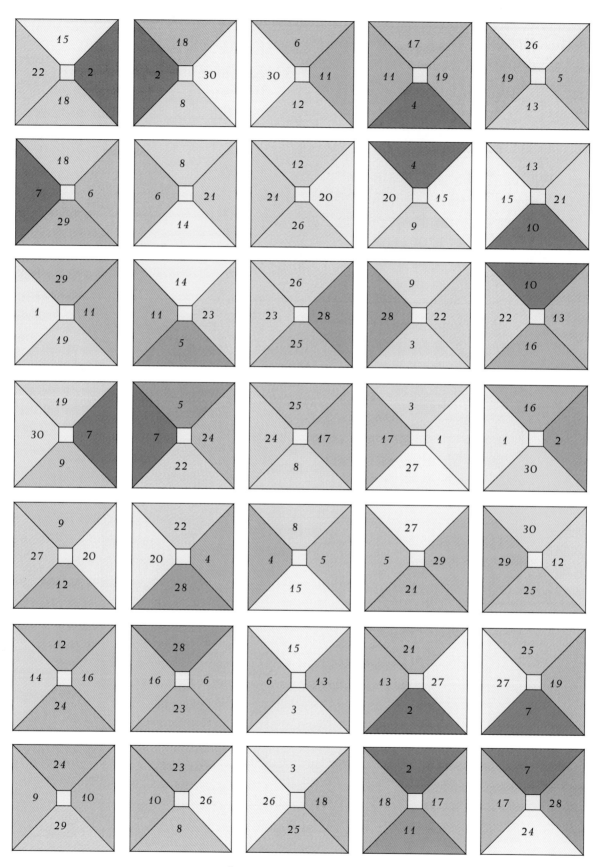

Butterfly Quilt Planning Diagram

218

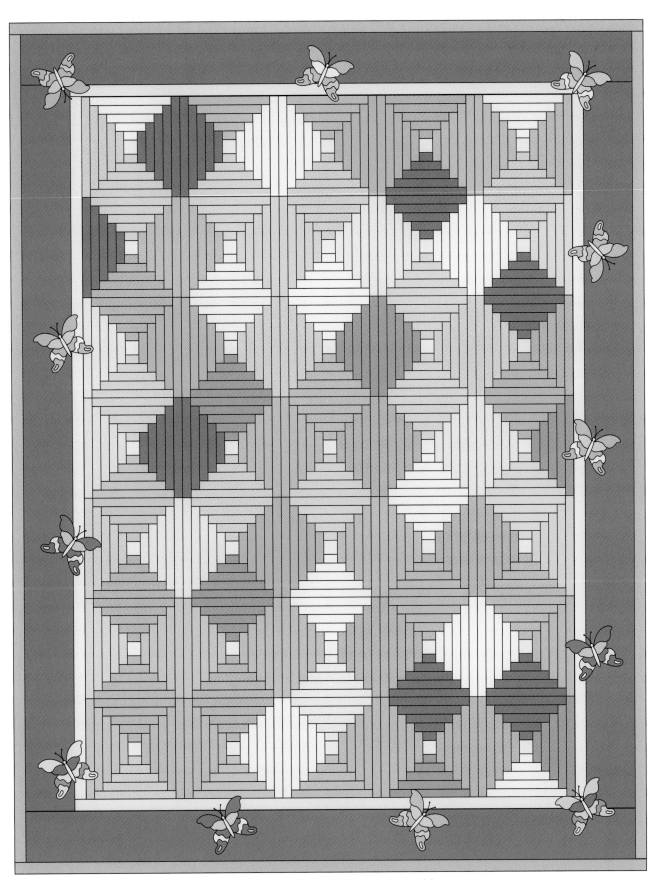

Butterfly Finished Quilt Assembly

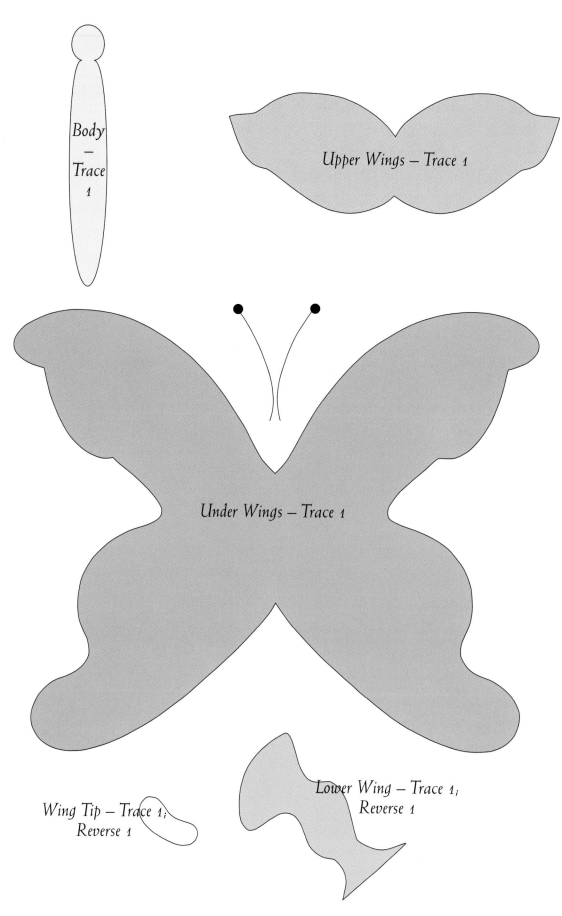

Body – Trace 1

Upper Wings – Trace 1

Under Wings – Trace 1

Wing Tip – Trace 1; Reverse 1

Lower Wing – Trace 1; Reverse 1

Butterfly Patterns — For hand-appliqué, cut templates 1/4″ larger all around.

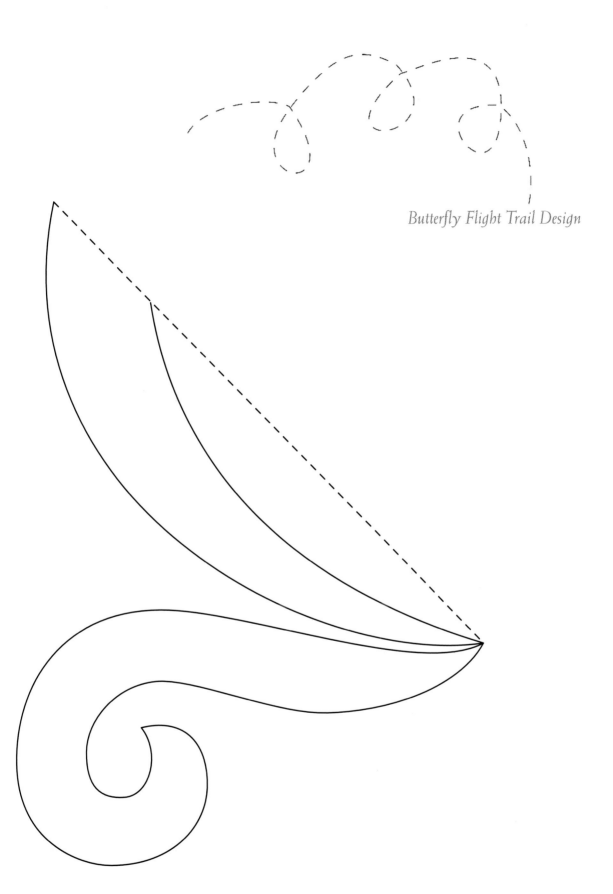

Butterfly Flight Trail Design

Butterfly Corner Quilting Design

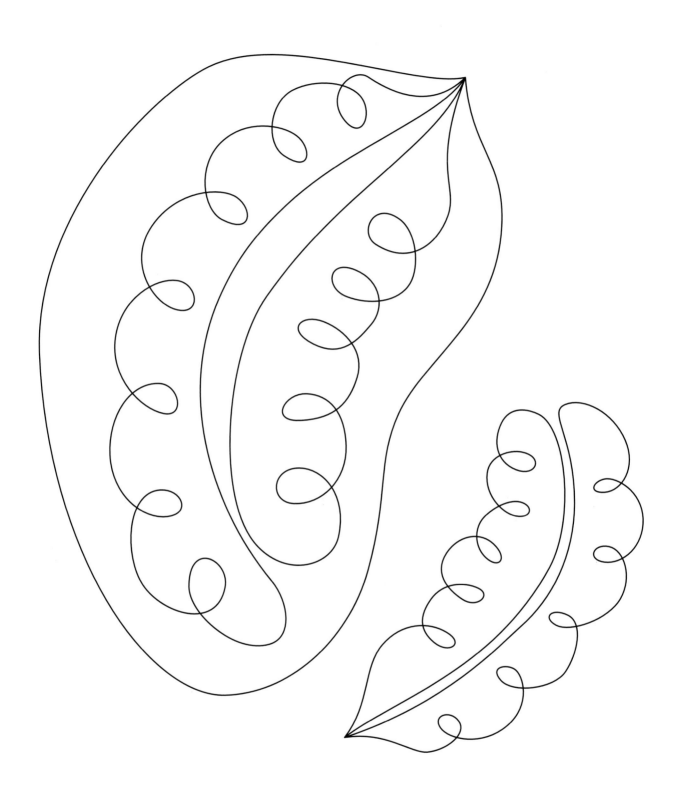

Butterfly Quilting Designs